LIFE UNDER THE SUN

The Unexpectedly Good
News of Ecclesiastes

HANNAH ANDERSON

Lifeway Press®
Brentwood, Tennessee

Published by Lifeway Press® • © 2023 Hannah Anderson

ISBN: 978-1-0877-8515-8
Item: 005842455
Dewey decimal classification: 223.8
Subject heading: BIBLE. O.T. ECCLESIASTES--STUDY AND TEACHING \ CHRISTIAN LIFE \ CHRISTIAN ETHICS

To order additional copies of this resource, write Lifeway Resources Customer Service; 200 Powell Place, Suite 100; Brentwood, TN 37027-7707; FAX order to 615.251.5933; call toll-free 800.458.2772; email orderentry@lifeway.com; or order online at *lifeway.com*.

Printed in the United States of America

Lifeway Resources
200 Powell Place, Suite 100
Brentwood, TN 37027-7707

EDITORIAL TEAM, LIFEWAY WOMEN BIBLE STUDIES

Becky Loyd
Director, Lifeway Women

Tina Boesch
Manager

Chelsea Waack
Production Leader

Mike Wakefield
Content Editor

Jennifer Siao
Production Editor

Lauren Ervin
Art Director

Sarah Hobbs
Graphic Designer

TABLE OF CONTENTS

Hannah Anderson is an author and Bible teacher who lives in the Blue Ridge Mountains of Virginia. Her books include *Humble Roots: How Humility Grounds and Nourishes Your Soul*, *Turning of Days: Lessons from Nature, Season, and Spirit*, and the recently released, *Heaven and Nature Sing*. Hannah's goal is to encourage believers to think deeply and broadly about how the gospel transforms every area of life.

You can connect with her at her blog **sometimesalight.com** and on Twitter **@sometimesalight**.

NOTE FROM THE AUTHOR

As long as I can remember, I've loved the wisdom books of the Old Testament—the pithy sayings of Proverbs, the emotional power behind the Psalms, and the unmatched pathos of Job. But the book of Ecclesiastes has always puzzled me. Since you're holding this study in your hands, perhaps it's puzzled you as well. Why did God choose to include such an earthy, contradictory, and even pessimistic book in the Bible? And how is it supposed to make us wise?

Over the years, however, I've come to appreciate Ecclesiastes in all its complexity. As life has chipped away at my naiveté, I've been comforted by the book's forthright manner. As I try to navigate each new season, I better understand why chapter 3 says that everything has its own God-given timing. And these days, more often than not, I find the Teacher's questions are my own.

So when the opportunity came to write this study, I jumped at the chance. And I am thrilled to invite you to jump in along with me.

Here in these pages, I hope you will find a way to make sense of Ecclesiastes that enriches your life and equips you for your journey. I hope that together, in community, you will find you're not alone in your questions, doubts, or fears. And ultimately, I hope that these weeks of study will spark new insights and new questions for you—ones that find their ultimate fulfillment in Jesus Christ Himself.

So that maybe, by the time we come to the end of the study, the wisdom of Ecclesiastes will shine in all its splendor, lighting every step of your life under the sun.

Grace,

Hannah

HOW TO USE

Welcome to *Life Under the Sun: The Unexpectedly Good News of Ecclesiastes*. This study takes an honest look at life under the sun through the eyes of the Teacher. As he wrestles with questions about purpose and meaning, you'll be challenged to see life as God designed it and understand your hope is in Christ and walking in His ways. In the end, we pray you'll find goodness in the life God has given you.

GETTING STARTED

Because we believe discipleship happens best in community, we encourage you to do this study together in a group setting. Or, if you're doing this alone, consider enlisting a friend or two to go through it at the same time. This will give you study friends to pray with and connect with over coffee or through text or email so you can chat about what you're learning.

PERSONAL STUDY

Each week features five days of personal study to help you dig into the book of Ecclesiastes. You'll find questions to help you understand and apply the text, plus insightful commentary to clarify your study.

REFLECTION PAGE

At the end of each week you'll find pages that provide space for you to process what you've learned, and journal thoughts you might share in your group session.

CALL-OUT BOXES

Throughout the study you'll find boxes with extra information to help set context, deal with difficult passages, and provide other information to enhance the study.

Extra Resources

◄ LEADER GUIDE

A free leader guide PDF is available for download at **lifeway.com/lifeunderthesun**. The leader guide offers several tips and helps along with discussion guides for each week.

BIBLE READING PLAN ►

An Ecclesiastes Reading Plan PDF is available for download at **lifeway.com/lifeunderthesun**. There are three options to choose from to help you read through Ecclesiastes.

Session 1

INTRODUCTION

REFLECTION

Session 1

Below you'll find some questions for this introductory session.
Be prepared to discuss these if you're doing the study in a group.

1 Is there a book you've read recently that you think portrays life as it really is? If so, what book and why did you choose it?

2 When someone mentions Ecclesiastes, what comes to mind?

3 One well-known phrase from Ecclesiastes is "there is nothing new under the sun." What do you think that means and do you agree with it? Explain.

4 What drew you to this study and what do you hope to gain from it?

If you're leading a group, check out the leader guide
found at **lifeway.com/lifeunderthesun**.

Session 2

LIFE UNDER
THE SUN

For many readers, Ecclesiastes can be a perplexing book. Not only does it appear to repeat and contradict itself, it also doesn't seem to have a direct or satisfying point—at least on the first reading. It can be disorienting and leave readers more confused than before they started. Because of this, we'll begin our study by orienting ourselves to Ecclesiastes as a whole. We'll consider its structure, purpose, main voices, genre, themes, and questions by focusing each day on the book's own introduction found in Ecclesiastes 1:1-11.

THE WORDS OF THE TEACHER

READ ECCLESIASTES 1:1-11.

According to the text, whose words will we be reading in the book of Ecclesiastes?

How would you describe the overall tone of this first section?

Does the tone confirm or challenge your understanding of Ecclesiastes as a book in the Bible? What surprises you about it?

WHOSE WORDS?

The first verse of Ecclesiastes tells us that we will be reading the words of "the Teacher, son of David, king in Jerusalem." But if we are reading the words of the Teacher, who wrote the words that tell us we are reading the Teacher's words? Who is quoting the Teacher? Exactly who are we listening to?

The question of "who are we listening to" is an important one to answer at the beginning of any Bible study, but it's particularly important when you're studying a book as complicated as Ecclesiastes. How we answer this question will determine how we understand the rest of the book. For example, when the Teacher cries, "Everything is futile" are we supposed to receive it as a direct, authoritative statement from God about life under the sun? Or are we supposed to read it as the observation of a human being that has been recorded in the sacred text?

To answer these questions, we'll need more information about the structure, context, genre, and literary form of Ecclesiastes.

Think About It

At this point, how do you understand the relationship between Ecclesiastes as the words of the Teacher and Ecclesiastes as a book that is both inspired and preserved by God?

THE STRUCTURE OF ECCLESIASTES

Scholars believe that Ecclesiastes is best understood as an example of frame literature or a "story-within-a-story." In frame literature, the main part of the book or essay is wrapped by an introduction and conclusion which is often voiced by someone other than the main speaker.

If you've read Mary Shelley's *Frankenstein* or watched *The Princess Bride*, you've seen frame technique in use. Both works open with a narrator telling a story to another person. In *The Princess Bride*, the writers chose to have a grandfather read the book *The Princess Bride* to his grandson. And even though the majority of the movie's action and dialog happens inside the fairytale (not between the grandfather and grandson), the movie begins and ends in the boy's bedroom.

In the same way, Ecclesiastes opens and closes with a Narrator framing the words of the Teacher. Here is a simple outline of the book:

Ecclesiastes 1:1-11: Introduction by the Narrator who quotes the Teacher's work

Ecclesiastes 1:12–12:7: Observations by the Teacher in his own words

Ecclesiastes 12:9-14: Conclusion by the Narrator who summarizes the Teacher's work

☀ *The Nesting Voices of Ecclesiastes*

With more than one voice speaking in the book of Ecclesiastes, it can be hard to know how they relate to each other. One way to think of the relationship is to imagine the voices as nesting dolls. Inspired by the Holy Spirit, the Narrator recorded and arranged the words of the Teacher. Or to put it another way, the core ideas are those of the Teacher but the Narrator delivers them to us under the guidance of the Holy Spirit.

Those who focus on God as the ultimate Author of Scripture can sometimes forget that the Holy Spirit used human beings to give us the Bible. Meanwhile, those who tend to emphasize its human authorship can sometimes minimize its sacred, life-changing authority. At the end of the day, the exact relationship between human and divine authorship is something of a mystery, but we trust that the words of Ecclesiastes—like the rest of Scripture—are simultaneously the words of the Teacher and the Word of God preserved for us today.

Think About It

What's the significance of God using human writers and common literary techniques to write Ecclesiastes? How should this reality affect our study of it?

Just as our physical Bibles are made from natural elements—paper, vellum, leather, and cardboard—the text of the Bible is made from the natural elements of literature. In God's wisdom, He used human authors to reveal Himself through nouns, verbs, sentences, metaphors, parallelism, and other literary devices. This means it's important we pay attention to how these elements work so that we can understand what the text is revealing about Him. Throughout this study, we'll specifically look at how genre and literary elements of Ecclesiastes work together to communicate its underlying message. Rather than diminishing the sacredness of the Bible, this approach helps us appreciate God's kindness to meet us where are. Our God does not hold Himself aloof; instead, He comes to us in our reality, using language, images, and symbols that we can understand.

WHO IS THE TEACHER?

READ ECCLESIASTES 12:9-14.

What textual clues in verse 9 suggest that the Narrator is speaking and not the Teacher?

According to the Narrator, what did the Teacher do with his wisdom? What did the Teacher write? Where might these sayings be found?

How does the Narrator summarize the Teacher's message (vv. 13-14)?

Ecclesiastes opens with the Narrator introducing the Teacher and his work. It ends with the Narrator summarizing the message of the book that holds "the words of the Teacher." But we still haven't answered a pretty basic question: Who is the Teacher?

Traditionally, Solomon has been identified as the Teacher. There are several textual reasons for this.

Read the following passages to see why some hypothesize that the Teacher is Solomon. List the clues given in each passage.

1. Ecclesiastes 1:1

2. Ecclesiastes 1:12

3. Ecclesiastes 1:16

4. Ecclesiastes 2:4-9

5. Ecclesiastes 12:9-10

Despite these allusions, however, the Bible does not explicitly name Solomon as the Teacher even though it does name him as the author of other wisdom literature. (See Prov. 1:1.) To complicate things even further, some textual inconsistencies make it difficult to definitely claim Solomon is the Teacher. (We'll look at one example later.) Consequently, the writer of Ecclesiastes technically remains anonymous.

READING ECCLESIASTES AS WISDOM LITERATURE

Unlike books such as 1–2 Kings and 1–2 Chronicles that narrate specific details of Israel's history, the goal of Ecclesiastes is not to provide a historical account of Solomon's life. Instead, it aims to provide timeless wisdom to the reader about how to live life under the sun. In fact, keeping the Teacher anonymous helps achieve this goal because the Teacher's wisdom cannot be restricted to a specific time and place. When we encounter a hard truth, we can't say "Well, that's just the way it was in Solomon's day." Instead, we must wrestle with it because it lacks a specific context. This keeps the book's message surprisingly fresh and relevant. The Teacher becomes a kind of "everyman" who gives voice to the struggles we all experience—regardless of where we sit in human history.

The Teacher's anonymity also invites us to partake of the same wisdom that God offered Solomon in 1 Kings 3:1-15. Scholars may disagree about whether the Teacher is Solomon, but they do agree that the content of Ecclesiastes is "Solomonic"—it is designed to make us think of Solomon and more importantly, to think of the kind of wisdom God gives those who come honestly looking for insight and discernment. It's the same invitation that James extends to us:

> *Now if any of you lacks wisdom, he should ask God—who gives to*
> *all generously and ungrudgingly—and it will be given to him.*

JAMES 1:5

As we delve into Ecclesiastes over the next few weeks, we're going to need the Holy Spirit's wisdom to understand its message and application. We'll face questions we didn't know we had and hopefully find answers for ones we do. With both Solomon and James, we must come humbly asking God to grant us the insight and perspective that we need. And when we do, He promises to give it in abundance.

ABSOLUTE FUTILITY!

The next step in our study of Ecclesiastes is to identify its overarching themes and repeated symbols. Today we'll look at the central image of life as a vapor.

READ ECCLESIASTES 1:1-11.

In verse 2, the Teacher makes a judgment about life. How does he describe it?

What examples are given in the passage to prove the Teacher's words about the nature of life under the sun (vv. 4-7)?

In verse 8, the Narrator repeats the Teacher's claim that life is futile using parallel—but not exact—language. What phrase in verse 8 mirrors the phrase "Everything is futile" (v. 2)?

How does the use of the word "wearisome" add meaning to the word "futile"? What extra emotion does it offer?

Having established the different voices of Ecclesiastes, we have another question to answer: "How should Ecclesiastes be read?" Literally or metaphorically? Are we supposed to passively accept the Teacher's words or should we wrestle with and unpack their meaning?

Part of the answer lies in the *genre* of Ecclesiastes. Unlike narrative books or the epistles, Ecclesiastes is wisdom literature and is not written in a straightforward manner. Instead, it uses figurative language and poetic structure to communicate its message. This is common for wisdom books like Job and Proverbs, but it also means we must do a bit of extra work. We have to learn to read Scripture literarily—to read it through the genre and literary features that convey its intended meaning.

☀ Literal Reading vs. Literary Reading

Recent challenges to the Bible's authority and inspiration have led to confusion about how to read it. In an effort to preserve the Bible's sacred role, some teachers have suggested a "literal" or straightforward reading that pays little attention to literary forms or structure. This "literal" approach can sometimes hide the text's intended meaning. Learning to read the Bible "literarily" or as literature, will reveal layers and depth we'd never see with a straightforward reading, and honors the fact that God inspired specific forms and structures to reveal Himself to us.

CENTRAL IMAGE

Thankfully, Ecclesiastes puts its central theme and main metaphor at the beginning of the book.

> *"Absolute futility," says the Teacher.*
> *"Absolute futility. Everything is futile."*
> *What does a person gain for all his efforts*
> *that he labors at under the sun?*
>
> *ECCLESIASTES 1:2-3*

The word *futile* is repeated throughout Ecclesiastes nearly forty times. Some Bible versions translate this phrase as *vanity* (ESV, KJV) or *meaningless* (NIV), but none of these English words quite capture the depth of the original Hebrew word *hevel.*

Literally translated, *hevel* means *vapor* or *smoke*. It describes the way mist hovers in the lowlands on cool mornings and burns away as the sun rises.

It's the fog that American poet Carl Sandberg describes as coming "on little cat feet.

It sits looking
over harbor and city
on silent haunches
and then moves on."[1]

It's your breath on a freezing day that hangs and hovers in the air before it turns to nothing. It's formless, empty, and void.

Translators render *hevel* as *futility* or *emptiness* to capture both the brevity of life and its mysterious nature. The point is this: Life is both short and hard to grasp. You cannot hold onto it nor can you completely understand it while you're living it. Like a vapor, it rises quickly, coiling and twisting upward with no defined shape or direction until it simply disappears.

Think About It

How does the Teacher's assessment of life hit you? Do you agree with it? Does it make you uncomfortable? Explain.

The book of Psalms (which is also Hebrew poetry) uses this same word to describe the fleeting nature of life under the sun.

Look up the following verses, locate the English word that corresponds to the Hebrew word *hevel*, and write it below the reference.

Psalm 39:5   Psalm 62:9   Psalm 144:4

In the New Testament, James also uses the image of a vapor to describe the brevity and unpredictable nature of life.

You do not know what tomorrow will bring—what your life will be! For you are like vapor that appears for a little while, then vanishes.

JAMES 4:14

But while the imagery of vapor illustrates the brevity of life under the sun, it also hints to the Source of our life—a Source that might just provide the purpose and meaning we seek.

 Poetic Language in Wisdom Literature

The use of poetic language is a feature that distinguishes wisdom literature from other biblical genres. One benefit of poetic language is that it conveys a lot of meaning in short, powerful phrases and words.

But poetic language also challenges the reader, forcing us to actively participate in unpacking its meaning and application to our lives. In a word, you cannot read poetry passively. You have to dig for its meaning. In the same way, the poetic language of wisdom literature invites readers of the Bible to become active participants in the process of growth. It forces us to slow down and consider the truth being presented. And thus, it seeks not only to inform, but also to transform.

HEVEL AND THE BREATH OF GOD

As we've seen, Scripture often uses the image of a vapor or mist to describe the brief, enigmatic nature of our lives. Our days on earth float away from us before we have a chance to make sense of them. This reality has curious parallels to how Genesis 2 describes the beginning of human existence:

> *But mist would come up from the earth and water all the ground. Then the* Lord *God formed the man out of the dust from the ground and breathed the breath of life into his nostrils, and the man became a living being.*

> GENESIS 2:6-7

So how did the life that began with the "breath of God" somehow become characterized as a vapor that flies away? And how does the use of *hevel* in Ecclesiastes point us back to God?

Part of the answer lies in the first use of *hevel* which occurs in Genesis 4 only two chapters after God breathes life into mankind. Thematically, the events of Genesis 4 happen outside the Garden in a world marked by toil, sweat, and chaos. It's there, "east of Eden" that we meet someone whose tragic existence represents all the futility and pain that life under the sun has to offer.

The Hebrew word *hevel* can also be transliterated *hebel* or even, *Abel*. That's right. The word that Ecclesiastes uses to describe our brief, confusing life under the sun is the name of Adam and Eve's second son. Why is this significant? Abel's time under the sun was short and tragic. He did what was right but still suffered. His own brother, Cain, murdered him out of sheer jealousy. Abel's life and name are both *hevel*.

Futile. Empty. Meaningless.

But that's not the whole story. Because when God confronted Cain, God said Abel's blood "cries out to me from the ground" (Gen. 4:10). And there it is: our hope in the midst of a life of futile suffering. Just like mist and smoke ascend to heaven, so too do our cries. God hears and He responds.

Along with the Teacher, we must confess that so often our days are *hevel*. But even here, in *hevel*, we have hope. Just as God was not untouched by Abel's suffering, He is not untouched by ours. And just as He first gave us life through His breath, we will be sustained by this same breath—all the short, vaporous, misty days of our lives.

Think About It

How has God shown you He is not untouched by what you are experiencing in this life? How is He sustaining you in your present struggles? How is He preserving your hope, if even in small ways?

GOT QUESTIONS?

Today we're continuing to lay groundwork for our study of Ecclesiastes. We've already considered the author, genre, and central image of life as a vapor. Today we're going to look at the book's central question.

REREAD ECCLESIASTES 1:1-11.

How is our earthly life described in verse three?

Summarize the question in verse three in your own words.

What examples does the text give as proof that it's hard to move forward or get ahead in life (vv. 4-7)?

Verse nine repeats the phrase "under the sun." How does this verse frame the problem of our earthly life?

Recall that this section is voiced by the Narrator. It acts like a foreword to Ecclesiastes, introducing the Teacher and the major themes of the book while giving us snapshots of what will come later in more detail. If verse 2 gives us a glimpse of the central theme (the futility of life), verse 3 shows us how the Teacher is going to search out wisdom: He's going to ask questions. And the first one on his mind is: "What does a person gain for all his efforts that he labors at under the sun?"

Q&A

You might be tempted to read verse three as a rhetorical statement. If you do, you'll automatically get a negative answer. "What does a person gain? Nothing. There is no benefit. Nothing matters. You work and work and work and have nothing to show for it." This nihilistic answer is why many people struggle with Ecclesiastes. At first glance, it seems the Teacher is saying life doesn't have meaning or purpose, so it doesn't matter how you live.

But we can also read "What does a person gain for all his efforts that he labors at under the sun?" as an honest question—in part, because it occurs at the beginning of the book. After all, if the Teacher's mind is already made up, then we might as well close up the study right now. Instead, this question will guide the rest of the book. We'll find it reframed and restated in Ecclesiastes 2:3 with the phrase ". . . what is good for people to do under heaven during the few days of their lives." And ultimately, we'll have to ask the same question about our own lives.

READ ECCLESIASTES 1:12-13.

What does the Teacher say is going to be the focus of his work? What does he give his mind to examine? (v. 12)

What assumptions does he hold about life at the beginning of his project?

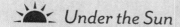

Under the Sun

The phrase "under the sun" is repeated in Ecclesiastes nearly thirty times and refers to life lived on the earthly plane. The Teacher's questions emerge almost exclusively from what he observes and experiences about life here and now. Only later in the book does eternity become a consideration.

As you read, try to suspend your knowledge and belief about the next life in order to enter more fully into the Teacher's questions and dilemmas. Try to hear his observations without answering or correcting them in your mind. This is an important technique to practice for several reasons: First, it will help you unearth the meaning of the text. Second, it will help you gain empathy for the struggles of those who do not share your faith. And third, it will help expose your own hidden fears and questions.

No matter how strong your faith, life under the sun has unresolved and unresolvable questions. Christian maturity means learning how to voice those questions to God, ourselves, and others.

INVITATION TO QUESTION

If the tone and approach of Ecclesiastes makes you uncomfortable, you're not alone. Throughout history, some have hesitated to affirm it as part of the Bible because of its forthright, unflinching nature. But by the time of Christ, Ecclesiastes was almost universally understood and accepted as Scripture.

Part of our discomfort with Ecclesiastes lies in our expectations—not of the book itself—but of the Bible. If we are accustomed to coming to the Bible for solutions, Ecclesiastes disrupts our expectations by leaving us with more questions than answers. In this sense, Ecclesiastes is an incredibly honest book, asking the kinds of questions we'd rather avoid.

But Ecclesiastes also teaches us how to ask the *right* questions. Throughout the book, you'll notice that the Teacher's questions and tone subtly shift.

In this way, the Teacher is much like Job, whose questions and posture changed when he finally encountered God in the whirlwind. In literary terms, we call this a *developing character*—or a character who shows growth throughout the course of a story. While the reality of the Teacher's circumstances don't change, what does change is his ability to live and embrace his God-given life.

One benefit of studying Ecclesiastes is that it helps us realize that our questions need to be refined. Again, it's easy to come to the Bible demanding answers. It's much harder to let the Scripture change our questions before answering them. But part of coming to the Scripture honestly means letting it rework and restructure the way we think.

Think About It

What does the role of questions in Ecclesiastes suggest about the role questions play in your own spiritual journey? Do you generally feel free to voice your questions to God? If not, why not?

Our need to ask questions is deeply embedded in human existence. So much so that voicing "whys" is among the first things children learn to do. Early on, my own children began wondering about the world around them. "Why do we wear shoes?" and "why do birds sing?" and "why is the sky blue?" Curiously, as we age, we sometimes lose our ability to ask questions—especially when it comes to our own lives and relationship with God. But like my children, Ecclesiastes assumes that asking questions is an essential part of our humanity. If so, then bringing our whole selves to God must include bringing our questions too. Even more, if God invites us to enter His kingdom like little children, I have to believe He means for us to come with all the curiosity and audacity of a child trying to make sense of her world. And just as we would never shame a child for trying to understand the life she inhabits, so too, our heavenly Father does not shame us when we ask similar questions.

QUESTIONS IN COMMUNITY

At its heart, Ecclesiastes voices the confusion and disappointment we experience in "life under the sun." None of us are immune to the feelings and questions the book expresses. But Ecclesiastes also offers a model for asking questions and processing our doubts together. At first glance, it looks like the Teacher is taking his journey in isolation, but the book's title and main speaker's name hold a secret. Both come from the Hebrew word, *qohelet*, which means "the one who assembles or gathers."[2]

In Greek, *qohelet* is rendered *ekklesiastes* (from which we get the English title of the book). This is the same Greek word the New Testament uses for the gathered church (*ecclesia*). Over time, translators kept the Greek title, *Ecclesiastes*, even though they translated *qohelet* from Hebrew to English as "The Teacher" or "The Preacher." What does this all mean? If nothing else, it means the questions and wisdom of Ecclesiastes was originally read and processed in community. The idea of "assembling" or "gathering" people together to learn wisdom about life is a deeply ancient rhythm and practice.

Unfortunately, in community has not always been a safe place to entertain uncomfortable questions. In fact, you may not yet feel free to voice your questions to others. But if Ecclesiastes offers us anything, it's the promise that a learning community *should* and *could* become this kind of place. As we commit to this study together, let's work to become the kind of place where the Teacher's questions and observations can be engaged, debated, considered, and processed safely.

Think About It

What makes you feel safe to ask hard questions and discuss difficult things? How can you foster a culture of safety and openness in your relationships and community of faith?

CYCLES OF LIFE

As we continue studying the introduction to Ecclesiastes, we're picking up the paradigms and categories we need to understand the rest of the book. Today, we'll look at the role nature plays in our search for wisdom about life "under the sun."

READ ECCLESIASTES 1:4-7.

In verse 4, the text contrasts the brevity of human life with the earth's stability. What is the point of this contrast?

In verses 5-7, the text mentions the sun's orbit, weather patterns, and the water cycle. What underlying shape do each of these share?

How does the cyclical patterns of the earth contrast the life span of a human being? What is the difference in their shape?

NATURAL CYCLES

After introducing the central question of Ecclesiastes, "What does a person gain for all his efforts that he labors at under the sun?" the text moves to focus on the created world, showing the difference between our temporary human existence and the earth's seeming timelessness. While our human lives are more linear, with a clear start and end date, the patterns of the earth cycle round and round and round, seemingly never ending. Curiously, these natural cycles predict the shape of Ecclesiastes. As we go through the book, it will feel like certain themes or topics are repeating themselves.

Structuring ideas this way is unusual for us modern readers because we tend to organize our thoughts from point to point, eventually arriving at a conclusion. But this circular structure reinforces Ecclesiastes's underlying message about the shape of life under the sun: Life does not progress neatly from point to point so much as it spins and cycles. We do not get to choose when we encounter different questions and so too, the answers we need are often embedded within our problems themselves.

Because Ecclesiastes does not progress in a straight line, this study will take a topical approach. Each week, we'll focus on a different question or idea the Teacher presents, tracing it through the course of the book. Simultaneously, you'll have the option to read Ecclesiastes straight through to get a feel for its cyclical nature. (See **lifeway.com/lifeunderthesun** for a reading plan.)

Think About It

How do the cycles and seasons of nature give us insight on the cycles and seasons of our own lives? How might our perspective on our spiritual journey change if we viewed it less like a straight line and more like the natural seasons we see in creation?

GENERAL REVELATION

Another reason skeptics have questioned the biblical inspiration of Ecclesiastes is because of how often it uses non-religious arguments. Today's text is a good example. In fact, you'll soon see that the majority of the Teacher's observations and conclusions come from what theologians call "general revelation." General revelation describes those things we can know about God by watching the world around us—things we observe from nature and human reasoning.

This text states that God Himself reveals what can be known about Him through nature.

What kinds of things does the creation reveal about God?

Based on this text, is nature a reliable source of information about God? Does this surprise you? Why or why not?

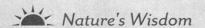

Nature's Wisdom

While the author of Ecclesiastes is technically unknown, the Teacher shares strong similarities with King Solomon, including valuing the natural world as a source of wisdom. In describing Solomon's own pursuit of wisdom, 1 Kings 4 notes:

> *God gave Solomon wisdom, very great insight, and understanding as vast as the sand on the seashore . . . Solomon spoke 3,000 proverbs, and his songs numbered 1,005. He spoke about trees, from the cedar in Lebanon to the hyssop growing out of the wall. He also spoke about animals, birds, reptiles, and fish. Emissaries of all peoples, sent by every king on earth who had heard of his wisdom, came to listen to Solomon's wisdom.*
>
> *1 KINGS 4:29-34*

The relationship between wisdom and studying nature is not surprising when you remember how often Scripture tells us to pay attention to creation as a way to understand God's work in the world. "The heavens declare the glory of God, and the expanse proclaims the work of his hands," the psalmist sings in Psalm 19. "Day after day they pour out speech; night after night they communicate knowledge" (Ps. 19:1-2). In our current culture that is deeply fragmented over the authority of Scripture, with fewer and fewer people affirming it, nature provides a starting point for connection and conversation across the divide.

Not far from where I live, there's a creek that's home to bullfrogs and egrets, muskrats and rainbow trout. But the waterway is probably best known as the setting for Annie Dillard's Pulitzer Prize winning book, *Pilgrim at Tinker Creek*. First published in 1974, the book details Dillard's search for glory in the natural world and has invited tens of thousands of readers to do the same ever since. While not a theologian, Dillard understands the natural world in much the same way the Bible does—as a source of both mystery and revelation. Writing about the truth that God has built into nature, Dillard calls us to pay attention to it so that we might learn what we might otherwise miss. "The answer must be," she writes of this general revelation, "that beauty and grace are performed whether or not we will or sense them. The least we can do is try to be there."[3]

READ HEBREWS 1:1-3.

In what ways had God revealed Himself in the past?

How has God revealed or spoken to us in these "last days"?

Verse 2 alludes to a connection between general and specific revelation. What word represents general revelation in that verse? Who does the text say is the source of general revelation?

Ultimately, general revelation and specific revelation are designed to work together like two hands or two eyes; and because they come from the same source, they reveal the same things about God even if they do it in different ways.

JESUS AND NATURE

During Jesus's earthly ministry, He often used nature and botanical imagery to explain the realities of the kingdom of heaven. He did this in part because His immediate audience lived in an agrarian setting. But He also used natural imagery because general revelation is open and available to the masses. You do not need a theological education or deep knowledge of Scripture to understand that when a seed falls into the ground, it dies to bring forth more fruit than it would if it had never been planted (John 12:24).

By using these widely-understandable images and categories, He was able to move people from general knowledge about God to specific truth. After all, when He spoke of that seed, He was really preparing them to understand and receive His sacrificial death and eventual resurrection. He was also teaching them about their own lives, how the "one who loves his life will lose it, and the one who hates his life in this world will keep it for eternal life" (John 12:25). He was answering the questions that Ecclesiastes asks in much the same way that it asks them.

Today, the average westerner does not live close to the earth and is less familiar with natural rhythms and patterns. But the power of general revelation is still the same. The One who made the sun is the One who governs all our weary days under it.

THE PARADOX OF LIFE

As the introduction passage of Ecclesiastes closes, the text becomes increasingly pessimistic about life under the sun. Ironically, though, this places us exactly where we need to discover the wisdom that makes sense of it all.

READ ECCLESIASTES 1:8-11.

This section opens with the Teacher rephrasing the "everything is futile" statement by saying "All things are wearisome." What paradoxes or seeming contradictions does the text offer to prove that life is "wearisome" (v. 8)?

Even though time passes, the text says, "there is nothing new under the sun." What do you understand this phrase to mean in this context?

According to verse 11, why does it seem like there is nothing new?

What emotions does this final section evoke for you?

As stated, the final verse of this section takes on an increasingly pessimistic tone, almost as if the cycles of the previous verses are now spinning out of control. The turning, turning, turning of the earth has become a chaotic spinning in circles, with rapidly accelerating velocity and centrifugal force. We're holding on for dear life. In this way, the Narrator brings us right to the edge and leaves us there, setting us up for the rest of the book and the Teacher's search for wisdom and meaning.

While passages like this can feel deeply disorienting, they do the necessary work of putting us in the right place to receive what's coming next. As it's been said, "You have to know that you're lost before you can be found." So too, you must come to a place of honesty about the difficulties of life before you can make peace with them.

Some the most profound spiritual growth I've experienced has come from learning to tell the truth about harm that has happened to me. I remember sitting with a counselor and telling him about a particularly difficult relationship and how it had affected me. He listened, then simply said, "I'm so sorry that happened to you. That must have been very painful." Without warning, tears filled my eyes as I choked back a sob. It had been excruciatingly painful. But until that moment, I had not had the ability or capacity to name it as such. Instead, for years I had soldiered on, minimizing the significance of what had happened, rationalizing it as 'normal.' And if not exactly normal, then at least "not the worst thing that can happen to someone." But once I was able to tell the truth, to name it as painful and harmful, I also found I could begin to make sense of it. And perhaps more importantly, I could finally invite God's healing work into my life.

Think About It

Why do we avoid telling the truth about the hard realities of life? How does denial act as a coping mechanism? What are the risks of denying life's difficulties?

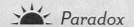 *Paradox*

Ecclesiastes 1:8-11 offers several examples of **paradox**—a seemingly self-contradicting statement:

- eyes that cannot see enough
- ears that cannot be filled with hearing
- time that passes but nothing new comes
- the past that is not remembered

The use of paradox in today's passage helps underscore the confusing and contradictory nature of life under the sun. Just when you thought you understood how things work, they don't work how you thought.

NOTHING NEW UNDER THE SUN

For the second time in these opening verses, the Narrator includes one of the most quoted lines from Ecclesiastes: "There is nothing new under the sun." On the surface, this is an easy claim to dismiss. A lot has changed since Ecclesiastes was written. Not only do we enjoy new technologies, we also conceive of ourselves in radically different ways. In the modern era, we're much more concerned with protecting personal rights, and we value individual human life differently. How then should we understand the statement "there is nothing new under the sun"?

At the very least, Ecclesiastes is reminding us that the more things change, the more they stay the same. This applies, in particular, to human nature. Our basic needs, desires, foibles, fears, insecurities, and questions remain the same. In this sense, the fact that there is "nothing new under the sun" lends credibility to Ecclesiastes as a source of wisdom despite it being thousands of years old. The words of the Teacher are just as pertinent today as they were back then.

What is the purpose of life? How can we find meaning and joy? Does our work matter? Where is God in all this?

These deeply human questions are not bound by specific time and place. The same things we wrestle with today are the same things the Teacher wrestled with thousands of years ago. And by giving attention to the *timeless* wisdom of this ancient text, we might just discover how to navigate our present lives.

In the end, this study may not reveal new insights or solve the problem of human existence; but it may help you remember those deeper, stable realities that undergird our life on earth. It may help you discover what C. S. Lewis called, in *The Lion, the Witch, and the Wardrobe*, "the deep magic from before the dawn of time."[4] Lewis, was referring to the timeless reality of Christ's sacrificial love for us—a love so deep and true it reaches back to the very origins of God's creative work. Or as Ephesians 1:3-4 describes, God "chose us in [Christ], before the foundation of the world, to be holy and blameless in love."

Think About It

In modern society, we tend to equate new discoveries and technological developments with progress. If it's new, it must be good. How does the claim that "there is nothing new under the sun" challenge this assumption? How does it temper our expectations about what's possible for humanity?

UNEXPECTEDLY GOOD NEWS

As the introduction concludes, it presents one final paradox: Despite there being nothing new, people don't remember the old. People don't remember "former things" (ESV) or "those who came before" (CSB). Our human propensity to forget helps explain why history repeats itself. We forget the wisdom that our ancestors learned through hard experience. So, we're destined to repeat their mistakes until we learn wisdom for ourselves. This is the human dilemma—unless we can interrupt the cycle by learning from the past. Unless we can learn from someone who went before. Unless we can learn from someone else's mistakes and successes.

Embedded in this seemingly pessimistic passage is a statement that almost dares us to prove it wrong: We will not remember what came before. But instead of forgetting, could we learn from previous generations? Instead of seeking only new developments, could we seek timeless wisdom? Thus, the challenge and invitation is issued, setting us up for the Teacher's entrance: Don't forget the wisdom of the past. Learn from the Teacher.

Curiously, part of the reason that we can learn wisdom from the past is because the ultimate source of that wisdom—Jesus Christ himself— transcends time (Heb. 13:7-8). While we hear the words of Ecclesiastes from the Teacher, we are actually hearing the words of God. And the One who is the same yesterday, today, and forever will guide us all our days under the sun.

REFLECTION

Session 2

Below you'll find some questions to help you think through
and apply what you've learned in this week of study.
Be prepared to discuss these if you're doing the study in a group.

1   **Which day of study this week was your favorite and why?**

2   **How would you summarize the Teacher's view of life under the sun?**

3   **How does this compare to what Jesus and the New Testament writers taught about life under the sun?**

4   **What are the main takeaways for you from this week and how do they apply to your life?**

If you're leading a group, check out the leader guide
found at lifeway.com/lifeunderthesun.

Session 3

WISDOM
UNDER
THE SUN

The age of Google® tempts us to believe that we know more than we do, which often hides our limitations of knowledge and education. But at some point, we'll learn what the Teacher learned: that trusting our minds is "a pursuit of the wind." How should we respond to this reality? We must embrace a humility of mind that entrusts what we don't know to the One who does. This frees us to continue to learn and embrace wisdom where we find it.

THE MORE YOU KNOW

Today we move from the introduction passage in Ecclesiastes to the body of the book. We're also shifting from hearing the Narrator's voice to listening to the Teacher directly.

READ ECCLESIASTES 1:12-15.

What biographical details do we learn about the Teacher in this section and what do they communicate to the audience?

What central question is the Teacher trying to answer (v. 13)?

What techniques or skills does he use to answer his question? (Look for action words.)

What is the Teacher's conclusion about life "under the sun"?

Having introduced the Teacher, the Narrator handed over the mic and exited the stage. The Teacher begins by stating his credentials: a wise, powerful king of Israel, ruling from Jerusalem. From this vantage point, he observes all that happens under the sun and tries to make sense of it. He watches, considers, and thinks about it.

In other words, the Teacher's process at this point is limited to his mind. He uses ration, reason, and logic to sort through the questions of life. What does he conclude? Life isn't rational, reasonable, or logical.

It doesn't make sense. And there's nothing we can do about it. Or as he puts it in verse 15,

What is crooked cannot be straightened;
what is lacking cannot be counted.

ECCLESIASTES 1:15

Think About It

What's your first response to the Teacher's conclusion that life doesn't make sense? Do you agree with him? Do you find his observation uncomfortable? Or are you finally glad that someone said it aloud? Explain.

CONTINUE IN THE TEXT BY READING ECCLESIASTES 1:16-18.

After failing to make sense of life, the Teacher reflects on his pursuit of wisdom.

How would you characterize the Teacher's trust in his own mind at this point?

How does the phrase "pursuit of the wind" in verse 17 echo Ecclesiastes's central image of life as a vapor? How might this connection be intentional? What feelings does it evoke in you?

Verse 18 says that wisdom and knowledge bring sorrow, and yet wisdom literature invites us to humbly pursue instruction. How do you understand this seeming contradiction? How can both be true?

As the Teacher begins to reflect on his own process, he uncovers a curious irony: If life is not logical or reasonable, then wisdom and knowledge won't be sufficient to navigate it. Even more, the Teacher reasons, gaining wisdom might even make it harder to navigate life because you will become aware of all the ways that life is irrational and disjointed. And so, he concludes in verse 18:

> For with much wisdom is much sorrow;
> as knowledge increases, grief increases.

Instead of doubting his own mind, the Teacher doubts the goodness of life and the pursuit of wisdom itself, concluding in essence that "ignorance is bliss."

Think About It

How does the Teacher's observation about the nonsensical nature of life challenge our modern assumptions about information and data? What role has learning, education, or research played in your own life process? What role has it played in your spiritual journey?

While this section has strong Solomonic overtones, there are some curious differences between the way the Teacher relates to wisdom and Solomon's relationship to wisdom. One difference is the Teacher seems to take a pessimistic view of wisdom. Despite having accumulated learning and knowledge, he views it all as meaningless and empty. Meanwhile Proverbs 4:7 records Solomon as actively encouraging the pursuit of wisdom, "Wisdom is supreme—so get wisdom. And whatever else you get, get understanding."

Another difference is how the Teacher says he gains wisdom. Based on this text alone, the Teacher makes it sound like he is the source of his own wisdom—that he has become wise because he "applied [his] mind" and "amassed wisdom." But according to 1 Kings 4:29, "God gave Solomon wisdom, very great insight, and understanding as vast as the sand on the seashore." Both the Teacher and Solomon had wisdom far beyond that of other people, but at least in Solomon's story, wisdom is understood to be a gift of God.

THE BEGINNING OF WISDOM

In one sense, the Teacher's observations about the limits of wisdom are correct: Because life is often irrational, reason and logic aren't enough to make sense of it. Further, the more we invest in knowledge, the more we trust it. The more we trust it, the more disappointed we'll be when it isn't enough. But the very fact that the Teacher is speaking to us as a teacher means that wisdom and knowledge are not completely worthless. It was worth it to the Teacher to pursue them—so much so that he feels like it is important to teach us what he has learned.

So an even stranger paradox emerges: *The wisest people are people who recognize the limits of their own knowledge.*

Facing the limits of our own knowledge can be particularly difficult in the digital age. I'm old enough to remember when researching a question demanded physical presence in a library. Searching through the card catalogue, pulling heavy tomes from the stacks, then flipping through numerous pages only to be rewarded with tiny crumbs of information. This would go on until I finally pieced together enough information to answer the question. Somehow this process both informed me and reminded me of how much I didn't know. Shelving books back in their appropriate slot, I'd see rows and rows of other books I'd never have time to look through. I found myself humbled each time by what I didn't know and what I'd never know.

Today, it's different. The same search take seconds. A note card-sized computer that fits in our pocket has replaced the library. The gap between what we *actually know* and what we think we know has shrunk to nothingness. So, we are increasingly confident that even if we don't know the answer, it's right at our fingertips. That is, until it isn't. Until life throws us a curve ball and none of our searches answer our questions about suffering, faith, doubt, and pain. In these moments, all the facts in the world can't make up for what we don't yet know.

As we continue this week, we'll delve into what wisdom can and can't offer us in this life. But before we do, we must acknowledge the limits of our own minds. After all, people who don't think they have anything to learn, won't. And people who deem themselves wise, aren't. But if we humble ourselves and acknowledge how much we don't understand, then maybe we can begin to learn. Or as Proverbs 9:10 puts it, "The fear of the LORD is the beginning of wisdom."

Biblical Wisdom Literature

PSALMS

Often referred to as the hymnbook of Israel, Psalms is a collection of poems and songs used in worship. The majority are songs of lament, thanksgiving, and praise, but a handful are more explicitly devoted to instruction and wisdom. These include Psalms 1, 14, 37, 73, 91, 112, 119, and 128.

JOB

The earliest example of Hebrew wisdom literature, Job recounts the story of a devout man who lost his health, family, and fortune, without warning or explanation. Like Ecclesiastes, it is concerned with the difficulties of life, especially the question of where is God in our suffering. Unlike Ecclesiastes, however, God plays a central role in the book and even has an extended monologue in the latter chapters.

PROVERBS

Proverbs is a collection of wise sayings attributed primarily to King Solomon and addressed to young people. The goal of the book is to give instruction and guidance for how to navigate life successfully. It opens with the famous promise that the "fear of the LORD is the beginning of knowledge."

ECCLESIASTES

The darker sibling of Proverbs, Ecclesiastes, concerns itself with how to make sense of life when it doesn't work the way you thought it would. If Proverbs gives us a positive vision for how to navigate life, Ecclesiastes keeps us honest by naming all the ways life disappoints us even when we follow wisdom. And yet, Ecclesiastes ultimately concludes the same way Proverbs opens: "fear God and keep his commands."

JAMES

The epistle of James is sometimes referred to as the wisdom literature of the New Testament because it offers real-world advice about how to live as a Christian. Like Hebrew wisdom literature, it is concerned with life "under the sun" and gaining the wisdom that we need to navigate it well. Reading James as wisdom literature also helps resolve some of its seeming tensions between faith and works by presenting wise behavior as the fruit of an underlying faith.

WISDOM SHINES A LIGHT

Having established the limits of wisdom, the Teacher reconsiders what wisdom can offer us as we navigate life under the sun.

READ ECCLESIASTES 2:12-14.

The Teacher returns to consider wisdom, in part, because he realizes that his successor will likely repeat past behavior.

> **How does looking to the future change his evaluation of wisdom? Why do you think looking to the future has this effect on him?**

> **In evaluating the relative advantages of wisdom, the Teacher contrasts it with folly. How would you define "folly"?**

> **What does the Teacher liken wisdom and folly to in verse 13? Why is this a good analogy?**

> **Verse 14 expands the metaphor of light and darkness, noting that a wise person "has eyes in this head." What do you think this means?**

As the Teacher considers who will succeed him as king, he realizes the potential for his successor to repeat the Teacher's actions. This sobers him, so he reevaluates the importance of wisdom. Given the choice between a wise successor and foolish one, he much prefers a wise one.

He reasons that wisdom is like light and folly is like darkness. Even though life is often irrational, at least wisdom allows you to look down the road in hopes of seeing what's coming. It's better to walk with your eyes wide open than to stumble around in the darkness. While wisdom and knowledge can't guarantee success in life, it's better than walking along with your eyes closed to both its pitfalls and opportunities.

 Walking in Darkness

The wise person has eyes in his head, but the fool walks in darkness.

ECCLESIASTES 1:14

In English, we have a proverb that connects foolish behavior with a lack of sight. When a group of people seem to be stumbling along in ignorance together, we say they are "the blind leading the blind." Of course, this doesn't mean that physical blindness indicates a lack of wisdom. However, the lack of physical sight does give us greater understanding into the nature of a lack of insight. In the Gospels, physical blindness is often linked to heart blindness or unbelief with Jesus presented as the healer of both.

GOSPEL CONNECTION

Imagining wisdom as light and folly as darkness is a particularly poignant metaphor for Christians. In fact, John opens his Gospel by naming Jesus as wisdom, light, and life:

> *In the beginning was the Word, and the Word was with God, and the Word was God. He was with God in the beginning. All things were created through him, and apart from him not one thing was created that has been created. In him was life, and that life was the light of men. That light shines in the darkness, and yet the darkness did not overcome it.*
>
> *JOHN 1:1-5*

Word in this passage is the English translation of the Greek word *logos*. This is the same root from which the English word *logic* comes, and here it means divine reason, purpose, or cosmic meaning. By using this term, John is claiming that Jesus is the very wisdom of God manifest in human flesh.[5] Later, in John 8:12, Jesus owned this identity by saying, "I am the light of the world. Anyone who follows me will never walk in the darkness but will have the light of life."

Something about who Jesus is and the way He lived revealed the true state of life "under the sun"—both in its brokenness and the hope of redemption. Something about Jesus's life and work offers meaning, logic, and light to our darkness. Like the wisdom the Teacher speaks of, the *Logos* of God opens our eyes to reality, revealing—not only the state of the world around us—but the state of our own hearts as well.

Think About It

Why do we sometimes prefer walking in darkness to walking in light? Are there particular challenges to walking in the light, despite its advantages?

The Teacher noted that both the fool and the wise person are destined for the same end: death.

List the two questions the Teacher struggled to understand.

Not only do both the wise and the foolish die, neither are remembered. What affect did this train of thought have on the Teacher (v. 17)?

Verse 17 again connects futility (*hevel*) and a "pursuit of the wind." What emotion or image does this evoke in you?

After conceding that wisdom does offer some benefit, the Teacher circled back to reconsider its limits. It's almost as if he was debating with himself, saying, "on the one hand . . ." but "on the other hand . . ." This kind of back-and-forth is common in Ecclesiastes and reflects the Teacher's thought process. Remember, we are viewing the Teacher as a *developing character* which means we will see growth and change over the course of the book. In passages like this where he seems to be contradicting himself, it also helps to read him as an external processor.

Taking up the question of wisdom, the Teacher again evaluates it in light of the future. But instead of thinking of the future of his successor, he considers his own future, including his death and legacy. He worries that living a wise life won't stop him from eventually dying or from being forgotten. If that's the case, what's the point of living wisely? What will it benefit you in the long run?

This section highlights one of the underlying tensions of Ecclesiastes. The Teacher is evaluating life "under the sun," in purely earthly terms. He is not thinking of life after death or leaving a legacy of virtue and influence. People of faith might find it hard to entertain this perspective. After all, faith rests on an eternal hope, or at least a transcendent one.

But for the Teacher, the value of wisdom is directly related to what it can produce "under the sun." His struggle: *Is it worthwhile to pursue knowledge, to walk in the light, to try to live wisely if you only end up dead and forgotten when it's all over?* In this respect, the Teacher's despair was entirely natural and even understandable. The apostle Paul affirmed this when he wrote "If in this life only we have hope in Christ, we are of all men most miserable" (1 Cor. 15:19, KJV).

But what if there is something else? What if the *Logos* of God, the one who is revealed as life and light changes everything?

Think About It

Is it enough for you to live wisely in this life if you die and are forgotten? How does the hope of leaving a legacy motivate you to live wisely? What role does your understanding of life after death play in your choices?

THE WISDOM OF GOD

In today's passage we'll see how the Teacher turned to consider his own mind's limits as well as the vastness of God's work in the world. Maybe the problem isn't simply that life is irrational. Maybe it's that our minds can't grasp all that God is doing.

READ ECCLESIASTES 8:16-17.

This passage opens in much the same way as Ecclesiastes 1:12-18. The Teacher speaks of applying his mind to consider all that is done on earth, but the tone is decidedly different.

How would you describe the Teacher's tone and posture in this passage compared to previous ones in this session?

Whose work does the Teacher observe in this passage that he does not observe in 1:12-18?

Besides having a different tone and reference point, the Teacher also reaches a different conclusion. Before, he was confident that life was futile, but what does he conclude here?

How does acknowledging the vastness of God's work in the world interrupt his thought process and change his perspective?

In your own words, explain the irony of the last sentence of the passage (v. 17).

In contrast to the other passages we've studied this week, here the Teacher is surprisingly humble, almost chastened. As before, he commits to exploring the world through wisdom, but this time, he observes "all the work of God." And almost immediately, he realizes how much there is that his mind cannot know. He confesses that he is unequal to the task.

Comparing and contrasting this passage with previous ones helps us see the Teacher's development. He goes from a confident, self-assured person pontificating about the meaningless of life to a humbled, awe-struck observer confessing that even the wisest people cannot grasp what God is doing in the world. The change is remarkable and brings about one thing: He shifts his focus away from his own work to observing God's work.

Think about how looking up at the vast expanse of a starry sky humbles you. Or how standing next to a thundering waterfall makes you cautious about every step you take. Or the amazement you feel watching a newborn take her first breath. Wonder. Reverence. Awe. These are the things that make us truly wise.

Unfortunately, contemporary society doesn't invite or support this kind of introspection. Instead, we live in a humanistic age that centers on human power and achievement. Instead of standing in awe, we celebrate overcoming limits and rapid technological development. After all, in just the past century, we have traveled into space, established global communication, and eradicated diseases. In such a world, there are fewer and fewer reminders of the limits of our control.

For me, gardening has become an important way to remember how much my life actually depends on God's unseen work. In theory, I can put a seed into the ground, water it, and expect it to sprout. Then, the sprout becomes a vine that eventually produces fruit. But as any tomato grower will tell you, there is a wide gap between theory and practice. Each season reminds me of my dependence. One year, it's too dry. The next, the rain won't stop. Another year, hornworms decimate my beautiful plants. Like so many things in life, gardening is the kind of work that forces us to the end of ourselves.

Despite our best effort, at the end of the day, we have to admit that it is God who gives the increase.

And so having considered God's work in the world, the Teacher comes to the end of himself. Humbled, he begins to understand that his own mind is not enough and entrusts himself to the One who is.

READ ECCLESIASTES 9:1a BELOW.

Indeed, I took all this to heart and explained it all: The righteous, the wise, and their works are in God's hands.

On the heels of confessing his own lack of understanding, the Teacher realizes the one thing that explains all of life under the sun: "The righteous, the wise, and their works are in God's hands." Yes, both wise and foolish meet the same end. And no, even the wisdom of the most educated cannot preserve them from the trials of life. Even the Teacher cannot make his own way in this world. Instead, the only way to make sense of life is to realize that all of it rests in the hands of Someone larger than us. So even as we pursue wisdom, we trust the One who is the source of all wisdom. We trust the One who is Wisdom himself.

I resolved, "I will be wise," but it was beyond me. What exists is beyond reach and very deep. Who can know it?

Ecclesiastes 7:23-24

☀ *Difficult Passage: Ecclesiastes 7:26-29*

Among the more difficult passages of the book, this section reads as a deeply misogynistic and arrogant diatribe against women. The Teacher warns against "the woman who is a trap" and claims that in his search for a good person, he only found "one in a thousand, but none of those was a woman." What should we make of this?

First, "the woman who is a trap" probably indicates a certain type of woman rather than all women. This would be consistent with Proverbs 5 and 7 that warn against the "strange woman" who leads young men astray. Conversely, we could also read these verses as the embittered musing of a character who is still in development. Surely a man who related to women in a promiscuous way (see Eccl. 2:8) can't be trusted to give us an accurate assessment of their value.

Beyond this, we must remember that wisdom literature often portrays wisdom as feminine. In fact, the book of Proverbs climaxes with a vision of wisdom embodied as a virtuous, noble woman. If the Teacher can't find a good woman among a thousand, he's obviously not looking hard enough. Regardless of the exact meaning of this section, however, it should not be read as God's judgment of the relative wisdom, virtue, or goodness of women.

WISER WISDOM

READ 1 CORINTHIANS 1:20-25.

How did the apostle Paul contrast human wisdom and divine wisdom?

Do any lines of this passage remind you of the Teacher in Ecclesiastes? Which ones?

Paul wrote that "the world did not know God through wisdom." What do you think this means—especially in light of the Teacher's resolution to find life's meaning by wisdom?

What's the difference in how the unbelieving Jews and Gentiles view Christ and how those who are called by God view Him (vv. 23-24)?

When God chose to reveal His wisdom through Jesus, the *Logos*, He chose to work in a way that did not make sense—especially to those who trust human power and wisdom. Instead of a palace, He chose a stable. Instead of Rome, He chose Bethlehem. Instead of judgment, He chose forgiveness. Instead of power, He chose service. And instead of reigning as an earthly king, He chose a sacrificial death. In the words of Ecclesiastes, it was all futile. Pointless. Empty. At least from a human perspective.

But then, who can observe all the work of God? Who can discover all His work done under the sun? As the Teacher says, "Even though a person labors hard to explore it, he cannot find it; even if a wise person claims to know it, he is unable to discover it."

As we consider the "foolishness" of the One who is Wisdom itself, we begin to see that maybe we aren't so smart after all. Maybe our calculations about the value of life under the sun don't make sense because we don't have all the data. Even if we did, maybe we still couldn't comprehend it.

Think About It

Part of the mystery of grace is that it doesn't make sense—at least not by human calculations. What do you find to be the most "foolish" aspect of the gospel? How does it undermine human certainty and show God to be wiser than all of us?

THE POOR WISE MAN

Humbled by observing the works of God, the Teacher reconsiders the value of wisdom for life. This time, however, he examines the case of the poor, wise man.

READ ECCLESIASTES 9:11-12.

The Teacher begins this section by reaffirming that life is illogical and unpredictable. He notes that skill and merit do not necessarily correspond with success and reward. Fill in the blanks from the text.

Being _____ does not mean you will win the race

Being _____ does not guarantee success in battle

Being _____ will not necessarily feed you

Being _____ will not automatically bring you wealth

Being _____ does not mean others will favor you

How does the Teacher illustrate and describe the hard times and unpredictability of life that people experience?

Think About It

How does the Teacher's understanding of success and failure challenge our own understanding? What particular formulas or life hacks do we count on for economic, relational, and social success? What role, in any, do you think "time and chance" play in our understanding of success and failure? Explain.

In verses 11-12, the Teacher challenges the notion that life rewards the gifted and hard workers. This can be a difficult thing to accept—especially for those of us shaped by "rags to riches" stories.

A "rags to riches" motif is one where the main character moves from destitute circumstances to wealth and favor. He or she usually achieves success through merit, hard work, and perhaps a bit of luck. While we might think of these stories happening in the realms of business or industry—like a Horatio Alger story wherein a poor young man gets an opportunity and works hard to build a financial empire—tales like *Cinderella* and *Pride and Prejudice* also fit the form. In these kinds of stories, beauty, wit, prudence, and good humor are rewarded with happy marriages and financial stability.

But in Ecclesiastes, the Teacher completely subverts the idea that wisdom and skill guarantee you'll get ahead in life. To prove this point, he offers an example.

CONTINUE IN THE TEXT BY READING ECCLESIASTES 9:13-18.

What was the city's predicament and how did the poor man deliver it?

What was the poor man's reward for his wisdom?

What did the Teacher conclude from this story (v. 16)?

Even though the Teacher technically remembers the poor man saved the city, there is irony here as well. The Teacher doesn't seem to know the details. He knows the poor man's wisdom was important, but it's almost as if the vagueness of the story confirms that the wise are forgotten. In this sense, the Teacher is not critiquing wisdom so much as highlighting how others respond to wisdom. Wisdom may have value, but don't expect people to see and reward its value. That's not how a broken world works.

So what can you expect of wisdom? If it can't make you rich, if it can't guarantee you favor or fame, what can it do?

Earlier this week, we equated wisdom's advantage over folly to the advantage of light over darkness. If nothing else, wisdom can open your eyes to the real state of the world. It can't clear or even choose your path for you, but it can light the path. It can reveal life's pitfalls and hurdles. In this way, wisdom can preserve and protect you while you walk.

Ultimately, this seems to be the Teacher's conclusion as well, even though we find it two chapters back. (Remember that the book cycles and circles like nature.) In Ecclesiastes 7:11-12, he says,

> *Wisdom is as good as an inheritance*
>
> *and an advantage to those who see the sun,*
>
> *because wisdom is protection as silver is protection;*
>
> *but the advantage of knowledge*
>
> *is that wisdom preserves the life of its owner.*

Wisdom won't necessarily make you rich. Other people may not recognize and honor you for it. And don't expect to be remembered after you die. But wisdom *does* offer a measure of protection in a chaotic world if only because it helps you see the dangers. And like the poor wise man, wisdom might just equip you to protect those closest to you—even if they can't exactly remember that it did.

I've been a mother for almost twenty years and I can tell you that young humans are not easily convinced of what's best for them. To be clear, I don't resent my children's questions, and I don't begrudge their challenges. If they engage respectfully, we have a policy of open conversation. Many times my children's *whys* have helped me grow in wisdom, giving me a better understanding of a situation. Here's an example I'll never live down: I forced my youngest to eat raw carrots for years despite his protests that they made his mouth feel "fuzzy." Eventually we discovered he was allergic to them.

At the same time, however, growing in wisdom means heeding the advice of mature, healthy people. Those who can help us avoid pain and suffering because they've learned from their mistakes. But here's the rub: children who are still in the process of maturing probably don't yet have the wisdom to recognize good advice. They are inclined to question and challenge, not out of rebellion, but precisely *because* they are still in the process of growth. As a mother, part of my own maturing process has meant recognizing this and learning to trust God's work in my life and the wisdom of my decisions even when my children don't like them (barring raw carrots, of course). Walking humbly together as a family has meant being open to their input while teaching them to respect and honor wisdom that they may not yet fully understand or agree with.

A PROPHET IN HIS OWN COUNTRY

The story of the poor wise man in Ecclesiastes 9 echoes something that happened during Jesus's earthly ministry.

READ MATTHEW 13:53-58.

How was Jesus's wisdom overlooked in this passage?

Like the poor, wise man, the wisdom of Jesus was overlooked by those closest to Him even though this very same wisdom brought them blessing. And despite Him being the very *Logos* of God. Speaking of Jesus as Wisdom incarnate, John wrote,

> He was in the world, and the world was created through
> him, and yet the world did not recognize him. He came to his
> own, and his own people did not receive him. But to all who did
> receive him, he gave them the right to be children of God.

JOHN 1:10-12

This begs the question: *If Jesus Himself did not gain wealth or power through His wisdom, why should we expect to? Why should we expect wisdom to guarantee us earthly success?*

Those who follow in Jesus's steps, who receive Him as the Wisdom of God, will often find themselves at odds with the currents of this life. Living and making such counterintuitive choices may lead us heavenward, but it is a narrow path that won't always be understood or honored. Indeed, living in such a way may lead to suffering and rejection—just as it did for Him.

But there is a promise here as well: While the world may not honor such wisdom, God does. Those who walk in this wisdom live as if they did not belong to this world at all. They live as if they are the very children of God.

Those who follow in Jesus's steps . . . will often find themselves at odds with the currents of this life.

SHARED WISDOM

Having traced the theme of wisdom throughout Ecclesiastes, we reach its conclusion in chapter 12 and hear the Narrator's voice again.

READ ECCLESIASTES 12:9-11.

What does the Teacher do with what he learned through his process?

Verse 10 says the Teacher wanted to find "delightful sayings" and write "words of truth." Does this connection between beauty and truth surprise you? Explain. What does this suggest about the nature of true wisdom?

What similes are used in verse 11 to describe the sayings of the wise? What do you think this means?

Having affirmed both the limits and the advantages of wisdom, the Teacher dedicates himself to teaching other people. He composes his own proverbs and curates the sayings of the wise (see chapters 7, 10, and 11). The book of Proverbs is a good example of such a collection, one reason why some commentators believe that the Teacher is Solomon.

Although these collected sayings emerge from different sources, the Narrator affirms that they come from "one Shepherd" implying they all have the same ultimate source. Some translators chose to capitalize "Shepherd" believing it is a reference to God as the source of all wisdom.

> The words from the mouth of a wise person are gracious, but the lips of a fool consume him.
>
> **Ecclesiastes 10:12**

THE STING OF TRUTH

The image of a Shepherd also connects to the simile in verse 11 that describes wise sayings as being "like cattle prods." Also known as a goad, a cattle prod is a stick with a sharp point that a herder uses to guide his animals. This image carries a bit of sting. Like us, animals can be stubborn and sometimes work against their own best interests. When this happens, the herder pricks or digs at the beast to keep it moving in the right direction.

In fact, this same image appears in the New Testament account of Saul's conversion on the road to Damascus. Confident in his own wisdom, the young zealot was intently and intensely persecuting the followers of Jesus. In a dramatic meeting, the risen Christ confronted Saul and asked, "'Saul, Saul, why are you persecuting me? It is hard for you to kick against the goads'" (Acts 26:14).

We may also find that the words of truth pinch. Perhaps you've found the Teacher's observations uncomfortable and disorienting. But as we receive correction and let these "cattle prods" guide us in the way we should go, we can be confident they are coming from the One, true Shepherd of our souls.

Think About It

What truth from this week's study has been the hardest to accept? Has the bleakness of the Teacher's observations left you feeling uncomfortable? If so, why do you think this is?

RETURN TO THE TEXT TO READ ECCLESIASTES 12:12-14.

Verse 12 includes an ironic line about too many books and too much study. What makes this humorous? What do you understand this verse to mean?

How does the Narrator summarize the message of Ecclesiastes in verse 13?

How do you understand verses 13-14 knowing wisdom may not be rewarded in this life?

Ironically, the Narrator warns against "the making of many books and much study." This is probably not a statement against intellectual pursuits so much as a warning against an over-reliance on human ration, logic, and argumentation. In many ways, this verse reflects the Teacher's observation in Ecclesiastes 1:18:

For with much wisdom is much sorrow;
as knowledge increases, grief increases.

Relying on our minds is an exhausting pursuit and, in the end, can't protect us from the unpredictability of life under the sun. Instead, as the Narrator closes Ecclesiastes, he leaves us with this final word about wisdom: "Fear God and keep his commands."

Yes, there are limits to wisdom under the sun. In this life, it may not be rewarded or remembered. It may not help you get ahead or lead you to financial stability. But in the end, those benefits may not be the point.

Instead, by humbling ourselves before God, we remember that His ways are above our ways and His thoughts above our own (Isa. 55:8-9). We remember that all wisdom comes from Him, so we follow wherever He leads, walking in His gracious light.

> Indeed, I took all this to heart and explained it all: the righteous, the wise, and their works are in God's hands.
>
> **Ecclesiastes 9:1**

UNEXPECTEDLY GOOD NEWS

One of the unexpected benefits of accepting the limits of wisdom is finding ourselves free to enjoy God's good gifts. Even if we could get everything right, there's no guarantee we'd be successful or be kept safe from suffering. In a broken world, we cannot trust our finite minds; nor can we trust the world to recognize wisdom for what it is. So instead of constantly monitoring every decision, hyper-vigilant against making a mistake, we must learn to entrust ourselves to God, remembering that even the wise are in His hands (Eccl. 9:1).

Perhaps this posture is what freed Jesus to live in both wisdom and goodness. Perhaps it's why those who trusted in their own wisdom never quite understood the way He moved through the world. In Matthew 11, Jesus addressed the fact that His actions were often mischaracterized and even condemned:

"The Son of Man came eating and drinking, and they say, 'Look, a glutton and a drunkard, a friend of tax collectors and sinners!' Yet wisdom is vindicated by her deeds." . . . At that time Jesus said, "I praise you, Father, Lord of heaven and earth, because you have hidden these things from the wise and intelligent and revealed them to infants."

MATTHEW 11:19,25

And then, as if on cue, understanding the exhausting weight we all feel at trying to navigate the world through our own wisdom, Jesus called to the crowds,

Come to me, all of you who are weary and burdened, and I will
give you rest. Take up my yoke and learn from me, because
I am lowly and humble in heart, and you will find rest for
your souls. For my yoke is easy and my burden is light.

MATTHEW 11:28-30

 ## The Power and Value of a Proverb

In this final section of Ecclesiastes, we gain a bit of insight on the nature of biblical proverbs. For the Teacher, a wise saying had at least three components. It must be:

1. Delightful or beautiful (v. 10).

2. Truthful and accurate (v. 10).

3. Compelling even if sharp (v. 11).

As we've already observed, proverbs are a form of poetic language that distills wisdom into a powerful punch.

But the poetic nature of proverbs also means they should be read as observations about the general character of life, not as promises, commands, or incantations. They are designed to be applied to the unique circumstances of our lives, but like any principle, they cannot speak explicitly to the exact situation we are facing. Indeed, knowing which proverb to apply is itself a matter of wisdom. Is this a time to "grab the bull by the horns" or to "let sleeping dogs lie"?

The gap between principle and application is part of the reason we cannot rely on our own wisdom but must humbly seek God in the midst of life's circumstances. While wisdom may be distilled in a proverb, it takes Holy Spirit discernment to unpack it and apply it to life.

REFLECTION

Session 3

Below you'll find some questions to help you think through
and apply what you've learned in this week of study.
Be prepared to discuss these if you're doing the study in a group.

1   Which day of study this week was your favorite and why?

2   How would you summarize the Teacher's view of wisdom under the sun?

3   How does this compare to what Jesus and the New Testament writers taught about wisdom under the sun?

4   What are the main takeaways for you from this week and how do they apply to your life?

If you're leading a group, check out the leader guide
found at lifeway.com/lifeunderthesun.

GOODNESS
UNDER
THE SUN

One of the stark realities of living in a wealthy and free society is that abundance does not actually deliver what we think it will. The more we have, the less satisfying each new thing or experience becomes. Ecclesiastes calls us to embrace good things as gifts from God and teaches us to view them as limited and temporary. We must learn the goodness of sacrifice and to "lay up treasure in heaven."

SEARCHING FOR THE GOOD LIFE

At first, the Teacher uses observation, logic, and philosophy to answer his questions, but in this next section, he expands his search for goodness from theory to practice. He moves from thinking about things to experiencing them.

Think About It

When someone talks about living "The Good Life," what do they mean? What would a good life look like for you?

READ ECCLESIASTES 2:1-3.

In verse 1, The Teacher decides to engage in a test or experiment. What was his initial hypothesis or theory? Write it in your own words.

How does the Teacher say he will test his theory?

Based on verse 3, what is the larger goal of the Teacher's experiment with pleasure and goodness? What does he hope to learn?

GOD SAW THAT IT WAS GOOD

One of the striking things about the Teacher's approach to testing goodness "under the sun" is that he still believes goodness exists. Although Ecclesiastes opens with somewhat gloomy overtones, the Teacher has not yet succumbed to complete apathy or despair. For him, the question isn't whether goodness exists but what does goodness look like? How can we access it? And what would it mean to live a "good life"?

In this sense, Ecclesiastes aligns with the larger narrative of Scripture about the nature of life. Yes, our experience of life will be deeply painful at times. Yes, it will be discouraging and sometimes even feel futile. But for all this, life under the sun holds good gifts for those who search for them. In fact, the earliest pages of Scripture set the frame for us, teaching us how to think about God's world.

At the end of each day of creation, as recorded in Genesis 1, God declares a blessing of "good" over the world. Eventually, the text climaxes with this statement: *"God saw all that he had made, and it was very good indeed"* (1:31).

"Very good indeed." This judgment is God's fundamental disposition toward creation, and it must be our starting point as well. The presence of trials and difficulties in this life cannot negate the fact that God created the world in goodness and sustains it by goodness to this day. Not only this, but God invites us to experience this goodness firsthand. Genesis 2 expands on Genesis 1:

> *The LORD God planted a garden in Eden, in the east, and there he placed the man he had formed. The LORD God caused to grow out of the ground every tree pleasing in appearance and good for food . . .*

> *The LORD God took the man and placed him in the garden of Eden to work it and watch over it. And the LORD God commanded the man, "You are free to eat from any tree of the garden, [only] you must not eat from the tree of the knowledge of good and evil."*

> *GENESIS 2:8-9,15-17*

Interestingly, the text seems intent on emphasizing the goodness and desirability of the garden that God planted in Eden.

Not only this, God also invited mankind to receive His goodness, even so far as to make partaking of this good, beautiful, desirable creation the very thing that will sustain their lives on the earth. Apart from one prohibition, God gave mankind all the goodness of the earth to enjoy freely.

ALL THINGS FREELY TO ENJOY

Lest we think the invitation to enjoy goodness is limited to the Old Testament, consider the following passages from the New Testament:

> *For everything created by God is good, and nothing is to be rejected if it is received with thanksgiving, since it is sanctified by the word of God and by prayer.*

1 TIMOTHY 4:4-5

> *Finally brothers and sisters, whatever is true, whatever is honorable, whatever is just, whatever is pure, whatever is lovely, whatever is commendable—if there is any moral excellence and if there is anything praiseworthy—dwell on these things.*

PHILIPPIANS 4:8

> *The voice spoke to [Peter] a second time: "Do not call anything impure that God has made clean."*

ACTS 10:15

Given what you know about how God created the world and the invitation to enjoy goodness, do you think it is inherently wrong to seek goodness and pleasure in this life? Explain.

What might be lost if we don't pursue goodness?

How does this affect your understanding of the Teacher's pursuit of pleasure and goodness in today's reading and throughout Ecclesiastes as a whole?

RETURN TO ECCLESIASTES 2:1-3. READ THE PASSAGE AGAIN.

The Teacher seems to express a level of frustration with his ability to experience goodness. What words or phrases does he use to describe his frustration?

How does the Teacher's use of the word *futile* connect to the large themes and imagery of Ecclesiastes?

Ultimately, the Teacher's experience of goodness is very much like our own. Yes, goodness exists, but life under the sun is a mixed bag: goodness and evil side by side, joy and sorrow together. Because of this, it's natural to become frustrated and disillusioned. The pursuit of goodness can feel futile and worthless. And often, the answer to the question "What is good for people to do under heaven?" is a loud, resounding, "Nothing! Nothing matters!" In these circumstances, we can easily despair and give up the search for goodness entirely.

In Psalm 27, David voiced this possibility by confessing his own frustration with life under the sun. After detailing his woes and struggles, he said, "I would have despaired unless . . ." (27:13, NASB 1995) Unless what? What kept David from despair? What kept David from giving up on finding goodness?

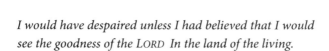

I would have despaired unless I had believed that I would
see the goodness of the LORD In the land of the living.

PSALM 27:13, NASB (1995)

What kept David from despair was his confidence that he would experience the goodness of the Lord *in this life*—here, in the land of the living. Here, under the sun. He believed that despite all the difficulties, life still held the promise of goodness because it still held God. So instead of trusting in goodness itself, we should trust in the God of goodness, believing He who made the world good will continue to fill it with His good presence.

But even this won't come easily—especially to folks who've known poverty or loss. When a person doesn't have enough to plan long-term, they end up focusing on the day to day. Curiously, even when a person moves to a place of abundance, it can be hard to change how they make decisions. I remember watching my great aunt, who survived the Great Depression, carefully cleaning and saving everything that came into her house. Newspapers, plastic butter tubs, and even aluminum foil stood in piles around her kitchen "just in case."

So in my own life, I've found it important to list out all the ways God has brought unexpected blessing into my life—especially when I'm going through a difficult season. It could be a new friendship, a travel experience, or simply finding something we needed on sale. These good things do not erase the hard times, but telling the truth about God's work in my life means telling the truth about His goodness. I acknowledge all the ways He has provided and cared for me so that I can learn to trust that He will continue to provide and care for me.

Think About It

In what areas of life have you been tempted to give up seeking goodness? Do you believe that goodness still exists in the world and that you might experience it?

How might God be inviting you to wait on Him—to believe that you might still see His goodness "under the sun"?

THE SOURCE OF GOODNESS

The Teacher begins his experiment by pursuing achievement, experiences, and all that his heart desires. But what does he find? What does he discover about the limits of goodness under the sun?

READ ECCLESIASTES 2:4-11.

List the accomplishments, possessions, and experiences that the Teacher gains in his pursuit of goodness.

Compare this passage to yesterday's reading of Genesis 2:8-15. What similarities do you see between the life the Teacher creates for himself and the garden of Eden?

In what ways might the Teacher be attempting to replicate God's own work?

Are there elements of this passage that make you uncomfortable? Explain.

While scholars don't know for certain who authored Ecclesiastes, the text seems to draw parallels between the life of the Teacher and Solomon's wisdom and glory. In the Ecclesiastes 2 passage for example, we see a wealthy king who builds public works projects (1 Kings 7:1-9), forces labor (1 Kings 9:15-19), amasses wealth (1 Kings 10:14-29), and enjoys multiple wives and concubines (1 Kings 11:3). The text does not tell us how to think about these things, but just simply states the reality of them.

REREAD ECCLESIASTES 2:9-11.

As the Teacher gains accomplishments, wealth, and glory, he does not lose his wisdom. Why is it important to the purpose of Ecclesiastes that the Teacher retains his wisdom?

From a human standpoint, the Teacher seems to "have it all." Why is it important to the purpose of Ecclesiastes that the Teacher enjoy all the world has to offer, including things that we might object to? What would happen to his experiment in goodness and pleasure if he restricted himself or didn't partake in experiences that promise pleasure?

According to verse 10, why does the Teacher believe he has a right to enjoy whatever he desires? Have you encountered this same reasoning in our culture? In your own life? Explain.

What does verse 11 say was the result of his experiment to test pleasure and goodness (2:1)?

After testing all the goodness found "under the sun," the Teacher concludes that everything he has accomplished is "futile and a pursuit of the wind." This is hard to hear, especially for those who don't have wealth or social privilege. After all, we may believe that money can't buy happiness, but we wouldn't mind at least testing that theory. But this is part of the point of Ecclesiastes, and why it is necessary for the Teacher to test goodness from a place of privilege. If *even* the wealthy and powerful struggle to enjoy goodness in this life, then maybe we're asking the wrong questions. If those who have no limit on their ability to enjoy every possible delicacy, gift, and human experience find those things unsatisfying, then maybe we're looking in the wrong place for happiness.

The Teacher's observation about the emptiness of riches is backed up by neuroscience. Studies show that once our needs are met (relative to how needs are defined by our current culture and community), having more money correlates to reduced satisfaction and overall sense of happiness.[6] Why? Researchers suggest that perhaps abundant wealth bumps folks from focusing on what they need to be happy to comparing their lifestyles to others, thus breeding discontentment. Or perhaps, having more increases the burden of responsibility. Regardless of the exact reason, increased wealth and accumulating things doesn't necessarily mean a better life. This brings us full circle, needing to rethink our hypothesis about goodness.

As it has before, Ecclesiastes is helping us reframe our questions before giving us answers. It's excavating and exposing our false assumptions to help us move forward. This explains the importance for the Teacher to experience everything that promises happiness, even things we would view as objectionable, like promiscuity. That such things cannot deliver ultimate goodness is not the point so much as the fact *that we believe they might*.

But this presents a different question: *If God made the world good and invites us into goodness, why don't goodness and pleasure satisfy us the way we expect? And perhaps more to the point, what will?*

While the text doesn't resolve these questions here, it helps us rethink our assumptions about goodness under the sun. First, note how the Teacher attempted to recreate Eden through his own work and effort. In many ways, he was successful. He cultivated a beautiful, flourishing estate and thriving community around him. And he viewed those things as the result of his own efforts, thus he

When I considered all that I had accomplished and what I had labored to achieve, I found everything to be futile and a pursuit of the wind. There was nothing to be gained under the sun.

Ecclesiastes 2:11

felt free to indulge in whatever his eyes desired. After all, he reasoned, "this was my reward for all my struggles" (v. 10).

You may recognize the phrasing "reward for struggle" because the Teacher uses it extensively throughout the book. But here, the context is slightly different. Instead of viewing goodness as the reward God gives to humans during their days of struggle under the sun, the Teacher views himself as the source of the reward. He is operating in a kind of self-reliant detachment from God while attempting to enjoy the very gifts that come from God.

Think About It

How do you understand the relationship between your accomplishments and your enjoyment of good things? Do you feel like you have earned the right to enjoy them? Explain.

A second way the text helps us rethink our assumptions about goodness comes via the phrase "all that my eyes desired, I did not deny them" (v. 10). We've already noted how the Teacher attempted to recreate Eden for himself, but there's another parallel with the Genesis account: the temptation to indulge in what our eyes desire because we believe we have a right to do so.

After God invited mankind to enjoy the goodness of the garden, He warned them against eating from the tree of the knowledge of good and evil. Soon enough however, the serpent tempted the woman by the suggesting that God was keeping goodness from them. The next words of Genesis 3 are particularly striking when read in conversation with Ecclesiastes 2:

> *The woman saw that the tree was good for food and delightful to look at, and that it was desirable for obtaining wisdom. So she took some of its fruit and ate it; she also gave some to her husband, who was with her, and he ate it. Then the eyes of both of them were opened . . .*

> GENESIS 3:6-7A

Ultimately, both the Teacher and the man and woman in the garden faced a choice: indulge in what their eyes desired apart from God or receive good gifts as from God. How they chose to pursue goodness would affect both their relationship with God as well as whether they could enjoy the goodness under the sun.

GOSPEL TRUTH

During His earthly ministry, Jesus spoke often about wealth and cultivating a proper relationship to good things. He warned that it's hard for the rich to enter the kingdom of heaven (Matt. 19:23-24). Possessions can distract and confuse us about what is really important in life. But in the Sermon on the Mount, he specifically addressed the tension between our allegiance to good gifts and the Giver of good gifts. "No one can serve two masters," he said, "since either he will hate one and love the other, or he will be devoted to one and despise the other. You cannot serve both God and money" (Matt. 6:24).

The question is not whether we enjoy good things but what are we asking good things to do for us? Are we trusting them to bring peace and happiness? Are we serving the gifts instead of serving the One who gives them? Ultimately, we cannot trust our own achievements, possessions, or experience to bring us the safety and fulfillment that only God can.

LIMIT OF GOODNESS

Over the next three days, we'll consider Ecclesiastes 5:10–6:9. Because of the poetic structure of the passage, we'll explore it in a nonlinear way, pulling out similar themes and ideas instead of moving directly through it. This section of Ecclesiastes uses the poetic form of *chiasmus* in which the main point or resolution is placed in the center of nesting questions, problems, or themes.

Structure of Ecclesiastes 5:10-6:7.

A: Wealth and good things cannot satisfy because people cannot be satisfied (5:10-12)

B: Wealth and good things are outside our control (5:13-17)

C: Trust God and enjoy whatever goodness he gives (5:18-20)

B*: Wealth and good things are outside our control (6:1-2)

A*:Wealth and good things cannot satisfy because people cannot be satisfied (6:3-7)

This way of structuring ideas is unusual for modern readers because we tend to organize our thoughts from point to point in order to arrive at a final conclusion. But the overlapping structure of *chiasmus* reinforces the underlying thesis in Ecclesiastes about life under the sun: Life does not progress neatly from point to point so much as it cycles and crosses back over itself.

READ ECCLESIASTES 5:10-12.

When we love gifts for their own sake, we risk missing the Giver of good gifts. This passage points to the foolishness of loving silver and wealth for itself.

What is the risk of loving silver and wealth (v. 10)?

Why might "the abundance of the rich" keep him from sleep? What does sleep represent more broadly in this passage?

The Teacher's focus here is not on wealth so much as how our desire for wealth can become disordered. What words or phrases hint to the Teacher's focus on this desire?

One of the ironies of life under the sun is that our longings cannot be satisfied by the very things we long for. Those who love money will never have enough. Those who increase their possessions will consume them and be left feeling empty—an emptiness they will try to fill with more possessions. And so, the never-ending cycle escalates: "one more" is never just one more and nothing will ever be enough.

To help make his point, the Teacher uses a literary technique called *metonymy*, in which a thing or name stands in for a larger idea. In this case, "the worker" in verse twelve represents those whose lives are characterized primarily by production while "the rich" represents those who lives are characterized by consumption. In real life, the categories are not this distinct and often overlap, but the Teacher is exaggerating the contrast to warn against trusting in possessions for happiness.

Think About It

Have you ever experienced "buyer's remorse" where you bought something you thought would make you happy only to regret it later? Looking back, why did you buy it? What were your emotions once you realized that you'd spent money on something that did not fulfill its promise of happiness?

READ ECCLESIASTES 6:3-9.

In this section, the Teacher turns his attention to the relationship between long life and good things.

How does this text challenge our contemporary understanding of long life and enjoying good things and experiences? How does it challenge our understanding of the relationship between work and retirement?

To underscore this point, the Teachers uses the image of a stillborn child to represent those who do not face the struggles of existence. What does a person who "does not see the sun" enjoy that the person caught in a cycle of craving and desire "under the sun" cannot (v. 5)?

What does the image of hunger communicate in verse seven?

According to verse nine, what did the Teacher conclude was better than "wandering desire"? What do you think this means?

☀ *Difficult Passage: Ecclesiastes 6:3-5*

For us, the image of a "stillborn child" evokes the deep pain and profound loss of an infant, but the text does not necessarily intend this meaning. Instead, the image is used to represent those who do not exist, in contrast to those of us who have to struggle with the realities of life. In modern language, we might communicate the same idea by saying, "It would be better if I'd never been born." We are not actually longing for nonexistence so much as expressing frustration at life. The imagery is stark and unsettling; but the Teacher is emphasizing the struggle of existence, not the very real grief of infant loss.

The Teacher ends this emotionally intense passage with a proverb: "All of a person's labor is for his stomach, yet the appetite is never satisfied" (Eccl. 6:7). Using the natural human drive of hunger, he explains why we cannot be satisfied with even good things. No matter who you are, you have to eat regularly. To eat regularly, you have to work for food. But every few hours, you become hungry again and so you must eat again. But to eat, you must work. And so the cycle continues. One meal cannot satisfy your stomach eternally. The same is true of our desire for possessions and wealth. Even if we get something that makes us happy temporarily—we'll soon become hungry for more.

One unexpected consequence of indulging our appetites is how it can negatively affect our relationships. In fact, much of what fuels discontentment is not simply a desire to have more, but a desire to have more than someone else. This appears in the most mundane ways in my own life and family: fighting over who gets the last piece of pie, proclaiming "it's not fair" when a sibling receives an unexpected blessing, or (being completely honest) the jealousy I feel when a peer receives an award or an invitation to a prestigious conference. *Did I actually want to be invited to that event?* I wonder. More often than not, the answer is *no* but the fact that I wasn't invited and he was, unleashes the green-eyed monster of jealousy in my heart. And slowly but surely, we come to see each other as competitors for finite resources instead of seeing each other as collaborators. And all the good things we do have in life no longer seem enough.

Given the insatiable nature of our appetites, the Teacher concludes that "Better what the eyes see than wandering desire" (v. 9a). This is an interesting statement because it repurposes and gives new meaning to a phrase we've already seen. Previously, the Teacher linked sight and consumption to our unending search for new experiences and pleasures. For example, Ecclesiastes 2:10a: "All that my eyes desired, I did not deny them."

But here in Ecclesiastes 6:9, the Teacher contrasts "whatever my eyes see" and "wandering desire" as opposites. Instead of searching for new things, it's better to focus on what we already have—what is right in front of our eyes. Meanwhile, "wandering desire" describes the restless nature of our desires. (Curiously, we have a similar expression in English: "wandering eyes" or "roving eyes" describes someone who is not satisfied with what they have and is always looking for something more, especially sexually.)

We see a bit of maturity in the Teacher. Previously his eyes looked around for new things to consume (2:10), but now his eyes look straight ahead at the gifts that he's already been given.

Think About It

How does focusing on the gifts we have help satiate our desire for more? Why does learning contentment satisfy us in a way that consumption cannot?

THE CHAOTIC GOOD

The Teacher continued to explore why pleasure, possessions, and wealth cannot satisfy. Having observed that people themselves cannot be satisfied, he turned his attention to how easily good things can be lost by events outside our control. How do we live in a world where goodness seems governed by chance?

READ ECCLESIASTES 5:13-17.

How does the man lose his wealth?

Why does the Teacher call this loss of wealth a "sickening tragedy"? (v. 13)

The Teacher notes the generational aspect of misfortune. If the father's misfortune was losing his wealth while attempting to steward it, what is the son's misfortune?

In verse 16, the Teacher again used the phrase "a sickening tragedy." What emotion do you hear in this phrase? Why do you think the Teacher was so deeply disturbed by this story?

Why is it particularly painful to leave the world as you entered it? What could it say about your life if you don't "gain" anything for your struggles (v. 16)?

In this passage, the Teacher tells the story of a man who loses his wealth through a "bad venture" (CSB, ESV) or "some misfortune" (NIV). His son, in turn, just misses being born into a family of privilege and abundance and is instead born to nothing. The man goes through the rest of his life "in darkness all his days, with much frustration, sickness, and anger" (v. 17), leaving the earth with the same thing that he entered it with: nothing.

The Teacher calls this a "sickening tragedy" (v. 13) because it suggests that our ability to accumulate and enjoy good things is governed by the whims of fate (as represented in the phrase "a bad venture" or "some misfortune"). The idea of fortune plays a significant role in Ecclesiastes and is central to the Teacher's thought process. Throughout human history, philosophers and thinkers have attempted to make sense of the seemingly unpredictable nature of life using the categories of fate, chance, luck, and fortune. Christian theologians reconcile these tensions through the ideas of divine providence and sovereignty, believing that the details of our lives are within God's care, will, and wisdom.

And yet, the exact relationship between life's unplanned events and God's will is still a point of intense theological debate. *When misfortune comes, does God send it? When good things happen, are they God's blessings or are they the result of natural consequences? How do we explain the randomness of natural disasters? How do we understand being born to abundance and modern convenience when others aren't?*

Interestingly, the Teacher appears to have a category for both fortune and the work of God in our lives under the sun. He accepts the chaotic character of life as represented by chance or fate while also believing that God is greater than both. Therefore, he reasons in verse 18, in a chaotic world, we must entrust ourselves to God to preserve us. Whether or not we share the Teacher's assumptions about the role fortune plays in life, we can share his conclusion that God is the ultimate source of whatever good we enjoy in life "under the sun."

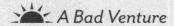 A Bad Venture

The phrase "a bad venture" in Ecclesiastes 5:14 represents a storytelling technique called reversal of fortune. In a reversal of fortune, the plot line takes a dramatic turn, plunging a character into a completely unexpected position. It can relate to unexpected loss or unexpected gain.

The book of Job, which is often classified with wisdom literature books, is devoted to exploring negative reversal of fortune. A wealthy, righteous man is systematically stripped of all he possesses. He loses his wealth, family, friends, and even his health—all through no fault of his own. While Job wrestles with why his misfortune is happening, the book does not resolve this question and instead refocuses attention on God's power in the midst of both suffering and blessing. "The LORD gives, and the LORD takes away. Blessed be the name of the LORD" (Job 1:21b).

The Teacher comes to a similar conclusion in Ecclesiastes 7:14: "In the day of prosperity be joyful, but in the day of adversity, consider: God has made the one as well as the other, so that no one can discover anything that will come after him."

READ ECCLESIASTES 6:1-2.

In Ecclesiastes 5, the rich man cannot enjoy his possessions because he loses his wealth in "a bad venture." But in this section, a person possesses all that he or she desires but still cannot enjoy it.

How is this person's dilemma different from the previous man's (5:13-14)? How is it the same?

According to verse 2, who kept the person from enjoying his or her possessions?

How might a person have wealth but be unable to enjoy it? Who will enjoy the man's possessions instead?

Even if we could be satisfied with good things—even if we found a way to relate rightly to our desires and possessions—we still cannot control all the circumstances around us. We cannot control whether tragedy comes, how long we live, or even our emotional capacity to enjoy what we possess. For all our struggle under the sun, we can be left unsatisfied. What are we to do?

GOSPEL TRUTH

Jesus pointed to this dilemma in Luke 12:13-21 when a man asked Him to arbitrate a dispute over inheritance. Instead of rendering a judgment, Jesus told a parable:

> *A rich man's land was very productive. He thought to himself, "What should I do, since I don't have anywhere to store my crops? I will do this," he said. "I'll tear down my barns and build bigger ones and store all my grain and my goods there. Then I'll say to myself, "You have many goods stored up for many years. Take it easy; eat, drink, and enjoy yourself."*
>
> *But God said to him, "You fool! This very night your life is demanded of you. And the things you have prepared—whose will they be?' "That's how it is with the one who stores up treasure for himself and is not rich toward God."*
>
> *LUKE 12:16b-21*

The parable of the rich fool reads like it's straight from the pages of Ecclesiastes. Instead of trusting in the Giver of good gifts, the rich fool trusted in his own wealth. He felt entitled to enjoy the goods he had stored up and planned an unwise business venture to secure it. In response, God demanded his life. All the pleasure the rich man had prepared for himself passed to another. Jesus concluded that the man's core problem wasn't the presence or absence of wealth but how the man related to God. In other words, our ability to enjoy good things in this life depends on how we engage and interact with the Giver of those good things.

Curiously, this is exactly the Teacher's conclusion as well—which we'll look at tomorrow.

EVERY GOOD AND PERFECT GIFT

Found at the center of the *chiasmus* (see p. 78), Ecclesiastes 5:18-20 offers the results of the Teacher's experiment with goodness under the sun. In a surprisingly optimistic tone, he concludes that we must receive good things as gifts from God.

READ ECCLESIASTES 5:18-20.

What does God give to a person as reward for that person's work under the sun (v. 18)?

According to verse 19, who gives both "riches and wealth" and the ability to enjoy them? How do you understand the ability to enjoy such good gifts?

What do you think the Teacher means when he says that the one who enjoys God's gifts "does not often consider the days of his life"?

Do you see growth in how the Teacher began his experiment and how he ended it? Compare Ecclesiastes 2:10-11 to help you answer.

The Teacher begins his experiment by indulging in every good thing his eye could see, believing that he has worked hard for pleasure and should have the right to enjoy it. But by the time he worked through the limits of goodness and man's insatiable appetites, he forms a different conclusion. In this section, he understands goodness under the sun as a gift from God.

But even more than that, he understands the ability to *enjoy* the gifts from God as well. In verse 20, he highlights a way of being in the world that is, for lack of a better word or phrase, lighthearted and free. The one to whom God gives good gifts and the ability to enjoy them "does not often consider the days of this life because God keeps him occupied with the joy of his heart (v. 20)."

This line is rich with *pathos*. You can almost hear the Teacher's longing. Here he is in a deep existential crisis, searching for goodness and meaning, while there are some who seem to be able to move through the world with effortless joy. They never feel the weight of angst because God has given them the ability to simply enjoy things. They do not carry the questions the Teacher does. They simply receive what they have been given and enjoyed it.

Think About It

Do you find yourself more like the Teacher or more like the person who "does not consider the days of his life"? What are some of your favorite things that God has given you to "occupy your heart with joy"? What brings you delight in the middle of life's struggles?

UNEXPECTEDLY GOOD NEWS

If you delight in good things easily, you may not understand the blessing you've been given—both in the physical gifts themselves and also in your ability to enjoy them. But if you tend to be more like the Teacher—you do understand it as a gift, but only because of its absence. You know how much you want to simply be able to enjoy life, to be freed from overthinking. You'd give anything for a light heart.

Perhaps the Teacher's own struggle with joy is why he repeatedly calls us to receive life and its goodness as a gift from God. For some of us, an act of divine intervention is the only way we'll be able to enjoy goodness under the sun. So, in its own strange way, Ecclesiastes offers us an unexpected kind of hope: The God who made the world good invites us into that goodness. Not only this, He draws us toward it even when we can't find our way. So that when we do catch a taste of it, we must savor it. And when we can't perceive goodness, we move toward it in faith—believing that one day we will.

While the Teacher invites us to receive happiness and pleasures under the sun, Jesus calls His followers to send their hearts' desires to a place beyond the sun:

> *Don't store up for yourselves treasures on earth, where moth*
> *and rust destroy and where thieves break in and steal. But*
> *store up for yourselves treasures in heaven, where neither moth*
> *nor rust destroys, and where thieves don't break in and steal.*
> *For where your treasure is, there your heart will be also.*

MATTHEW 6:19-21

It is good to be tired and wearied by the futile search after the true good, that we may stretch out our arms to the Redeemer.[7]

Blaise Pascal

Embedded in these words of hope is the belief that goodness is possible—if not in this life, then in the next. As we orient our hopes and desires toward heaven, we put ourselves in the place to receive the goodness that God promises to shower down on us. As James puts it,

> *Every good and perfect gift is from above, coming down from*
> *the Father of lights, who does not change like shifting shadows.*

JAMES 1:17

Don't miss what's going on here. Life under the sun is vaporous and shadow-like. And yet, God, who is Light, does not change like shifting shadows. He is a stable Giver of goodness who pours it down on us like rain. Like children in a rainstorm, we lift our tear-streaked faces to Him, opening our mouths wide to catch whatever drops may fall.

Think About It

Have you ever experienced a season when things you normally enjoyed did not bring you happiness? What was happening in that season? How did you feel God's presence or absence in it?

REFLECTION

Session 4

Below you'll find some questions to help you think through
and apply what you've learned in this week of study.
Be prepared to discuss these if you're doing the study in a group.

1 Which day of study this week was your favorite and why?

2 How would you summarize the Teacher's view of goodness under the sun?

3 How does this compare to what Jesus and the New Testament writers taught about goodness under the sun?

4 What are the main takeaways for you from this week and how do they apply to your life?

If you're leading a group, check out the leader guide
found at lifeway.com/lifeunderthesun.

Session 5

WORKING UNDER THE SUN

In the modern west, we tend to value people based on what they produce and contribute to society. We love stories of folks who rise from rags to riches through sheer determination and hard work. And whether it's a new productivity app or the opportunity to join a new venture "at the ground floor," we firmly believe that work can solve our most pressing problems. But do our expectations line up with reality? Does work deliver what we expect? And how should we respond when our work disappoints us?

WORKING UNDER THE SUN

After the Teacher considers the limits of pleasure and knowledge, he turns his attention to work. Maybe the way to find satisfaction and meaning in this life is through hard work and productivity. Maybe if we just commit ourselves, find the right career path, hack our habits, and hustle, we can find the stability and peace we long for.

Think About It

What messages have you received about work? What is your understanding of the relationship between work and happiness?

READ ECCLESIASTES 1:1-3.

Based on these verses, how would you describe the Teacher's attitude toward work?

How does the Teacher's perspective challenge what you think the Scripture teaches about work?

IN THE BEGINNING

The first time the Bible references human work is immediately after God created man and woman.

> So God created man
> in his own image;
> he created him in the image of God;
> he created them male and female.
> God blessed them, and God said to them, "Be fruitful, multiply,
> fill the earth, and subdue it. Rule the fish of the sea, the birds
> of the sky, and every creature that crawls on the earth."

GENESIS 1:27-28

Theologians refer to verse 28 as the creation mandate—God calling human beings to steward the earth. These verses should be read holistically: the work of family is interdependent with the work of ruling over the earth. In God's economy, there is no separation between the work that happens in the home and the work that happens in more public spaces. All work is valuable, and all work reflects God's creative nature.

What do you infer from the fact that Scripture ties our identity as image bearers to our work?

What are some potential pitfalls in relating our identity with our work? How might a good thing become warped?

God is an active, creative God. As people made in His image, we are called to be active, creative people. We work because God works.

Genesis 2 communicates another fundamental truth about human work:

> The LORD God planted a garden in Eden in the east, and there he
> placed the man he had formed. The LORD God caused to grow out
> of the ground every tree pleasing in appearance and good for food,
> including the tree of life in the middle of the garden, as well as the tree
> of the knowledge of good and evil . . . The LORD God took the man and
> placed him in the garden of Eden to work it and watch over it. And
> the LORD God commanded the man, "You are free to eat from any tree
> of the garden, but you must not eat from the tree of the knowledge of
> good and evil, for on the day you eat from it, you will certainly die."

GENESIS 2:8-9,15-17

What work did God give the man to do?

Based on this passage, what can you infer about the relationship
between the man's work and how he will be sustained in the world?

Who is the source of both the man's work and his provision?

As humanity stewards the earth through their work, they will reap
benefit from the earth in the form of food, provision, shelter, and care.
But if working is a gift from God and it sustains us, why does the Teacher
take such a dim view of it?

Remember the Teacher is speaking about life "under the sun." He is dealing
with the world as it is, not as it was created or as we hope it might be. When

the Teacher speaks of human work as futile and pointless, he is echoing the words of Genesis 3:17b-19:

> *The ground is cursed because of you.*
> *You will eat from it by means of painful labor*
> *all the days of your life.*
> *It will produce thorns and thistles for you,*
> *and you will eat the plants of the field.*
> *You will eat bread by the sweat of your brow/*
> *until you return to the ground,*
> *since you were taken from it.*
> *For you are dust,*
> *and you will return to dust.*

Spoken after the man and woman eat from the tree of the knowledge of good and evil, this passage describes how sin's presence affects the work we do.

What phrases or words does the text use to describe work now?

How do these words and phrases translate for our society and work culture where the majority do not engage in agriculture?

What particular difficulties do you face in your own work?

If we're honest, most of us would admit that work can be discouraging and disappointing at times. Even when we love what we do and do it well, it can be exhausting. Especially when we invest a great deal of time, energy, and resources in a project only to see it whither on the vine.

This reality hit home for us the summer we planted some heirloom pole beans. These seeds had been passed down in my husband's mountain community for years, and it was finally our turn to cultivate them. After carefully preparing the soil and building stakes, we lovingly planted them. Soon enough, the beans sprouted and with them, our hopes. We tended them carefully. For us, these beans were more than food to accent a meal—they were generations in the making, and we saw ourselves as stewards of their unique properties. As the stalks began to climb, however, a strange thing happened. Beautiful lush vines wrapped around the stakes; hundreds of thick green leaves unfurled; and yet, no blossoms appeared. The plants looked healthy and vibrant, but no blossoms meant no beans. And no beans meant both nothing to eat and nothing to pass on. The worst part is that there was no explanation for it. We had done everything we knew to do. The weather had been fine. No pests had attacked them. The beans simply didn't bloom.

Thankfully, friends and family had also cultivated the beans that year so the future of the line did not depend solely on our blossomless plants. But we felt a particular helplessness that summer. If you work hard to do everything you're supposed to do, shouldn't you at least get beans? Shouldn't you have the right to expect a reward? If not, why even try? With no guarantees, what's the point?

> My Father is still working, and I am working also.
>
> **John 5:17**

But this pointless, exhausting world is the same world Jesus entered. It is the world in which He Himself began working as a young boy, laboring as a carpenter, covered in dust and grime for decades before He began His recorded ministry. It is the world He came to redeem through His life and death. So that even in the face of opposition and discouragement, He could say in John 5:17, "My Father is still working, and I am working also."

And ultimately, Jesus's commitment to finish the work that the Father had given Him would result in the redemption of our work as well.

WORKING FOR GOD

In today's passage, the Teacher goes into more specific details about the futility and pointlessness of human work—especially working with other people.

READ ECCLESIASTES 2:18-23.

What are the Teacher's thoughts and feelings about having to turn his work over to someone else (vv. 18-19)?

What words does he use to convey his frustration over people often getting credit for work they haven't done (vv. 21-22)?

How does the Teacher feel about being unable to protect his work—both from those who would destroy it and from those who would take credit for it? Do you think his response is justified (vv. 22-23)?

What exactly is the Teacher wrestling with in this passage? What might he be tempted to do because of it?

In many ways, the Teacher is expressing the helplessness we all feel when we realize that our work is affected by things outside our control. Muddy footprints across your newly washed kitchen floor. A coworker getting credit for the report that you created. The unexpected market crash that guts your retirement. Each of these things, in their own way, tempts us to despair and tells us working hard just isn't worth it.

Think About It

How are you tempted to respond when your careful work is ruined by someone else? Or when someone else gets credit for your work? What does despair whisper to you in these moments?

Our inability to protect our work is one of the very real thorns of life under the sun. Left alone with our work, it's easy to understand the Teacher's sense of hopelessness. If our work begins and ends with us, it's easy to understand the Teacher's despair. But what if we're not alone in our work?

READ ECCLESIASTES 2:24-26.

How does knowing your work comes from God help you continue in it despite the thorns that surround it?

In verse 25, the Teacher says that it is impossible to enjoy life (including our work) apart from God. Based on what we learned yesterday, why does this make sense?

What is the Teacher's response to the way God seemingly distributes resources based on something other than our hard work (v. 26)? Does this passage seem fair to you? Explain.

Even from his limited perspective, the Teacher knows we cannot enjoy our work apart from God. But here in verse 26, he makes another observation. To him, God appears to distribute reward based on something other than human effort. Despite "gathering and accumulating," the sinner ends up giving the fruit of his labor to others. Initially, the Teacher sees this as problematic claiming that it is "futile and a pursuit of the wind." After all, if you can't count on your own work—sinner or no—what can you count on? Are we really that dependent? And who among us can claim to perfectly please God?

While we don't get answers to those questions here, the Teacher takes the first steps toward resolution by questioning his initial understanding of work. He reorients his view away from human effort to center God in his understanding. Even though he may not fully comprehend it, he's discovering that human work and whatever follows it can't be explained apart from God. And whether he knows it or not, the Teacher echoes wisdom that Jesus would embody Himself one day.

GOSPEL TRUTH

The earliest recorded statement about how Jesus viewed His work occurs in Luke 2:49, when as a young boy, He remained in the temple to converse with the teachers. When His parents finally found Him, Mary asked why He thought He could stay behind. In response, Jesus said, "Didn't you know that it was necessary for me to be in my Father's house?"

The phrase, "In my Father's house" can also be translated "about my Father's business" or "doing my Father's work" and suggests that even at a young age, Jesus understood His work as coming from God. Later, during His public ministry, He would reiterate this same idea.

Look up the following verses, and write how Jesus described His work:

John 4:34

The Latin phrase *coram Deo* literally translates *before the face of God* and is used by Christians to describe how we live our lives and do our work in God's presence. Whatever we are called to do, we do it first and foremost for Him.

John 6:38

John 12:49

This singular vision and deep sense of having received His work from the Father sheltered Jesus from the pressure and anxieties that can accompany work under the sun. It did not necessarily make His calling easier, but it changed the frame of reference. The most important thing for Jesus was not pleasing other people or even accomplishing certain goals. The most important thing was Who he was working for.

By trusting Himself and His work to the Father, Jesus could rest safely in the Father's care—no matter what happened.

 Sagrada Família

In the Eixample district of Barcelona, Spain, a magnificent cathedral rises from the earth. Begun in 1882, the Sagrada Família ("Church of the Sacred Family") has been under construction for nearly 150 years. It is the creation of chief architect, Antoni Gaudí, a devout Christian who viewed his creative work as both coming from God and informed by God's own. When over the years, folks would wonder about the long period of construction, Gaudí is reported to have replied, "My client is not in a hurry."

When Gaudí died in 1926, the Sagrada Família was roughly twenty percent completed. He was buried in the church's crypt, and in this deeply poetic way, Gaudí's work continues to grow around him to this day.[8]

WORKING WITH GOD

In today's passage, the Teacher returns to his original question, "What does the worker gain from his struggles?" But this time instead of focusing on human partners, he tries to make sense of human work in light of God's work.

READ ECCLESIASTES 3:9-15.

How does the Teacher describe human work in verse 10? How does it compare to how Genesis describes human vocation in Genesis 2?

How did the Teacher describe God's work?

While the Teacher acknowledged that God's work is unknowable and will last forever, this didn't seem to inspire him in his own work. What words or phrases in verses 14-15 point to this?

How would you describe the Teacher's attitude toward human work as compared to God's work?

While the Teacher was moving closer to understanding work *coram Deo*, it's understandable if you read a hint of fatalism in his words. Returning to the original question, "What does the worker gain from his struggles?" the answer seems to be, "Nothing! God is going to do what God is going to do. Your work can't change what's going to happen so you might as well enjoy the ride."

At the same time, the Teacher's tone is much more optimistic than before. Even as he accepts the limits of what his work can and can't do under the sun, this opens him up to enjoy goodness. In verse 13, he values simple gifts like eating and drinking and just enjoying the process of work itself.

GOSPEL TRUTH

As with his other observations, the Teacher is hitting on truth even though it's not fully revealed. In one sense, the fact that God's work does not depend on us relieves a great deal of pressure. Furthermore, believing that God can accomplish His work independently of us is foundational to trusting Him for salvation. In Ephesians 2, Paul wrote,

> *For you are saved by grace through faith, and this is not from yourselves;*
> *it is God's gift—not from works, so that no one can boast.*

EPHESIANS 2:8-9

Part of trusting the finished work of Jesus means knowing we cannot do this work ourselves. We are helpless, dependent creatures who throw ourselves on the mercy of our loving, kind God.

At the same time, it's natural to want to know that our work in this life has purpose and meaning. We want to know that God isn't just playing with us or giving us work to keep us "occupied." We want to know that our work matters. Perhaps that's why Paul further explained in the very next verse,

> *For we are his workmanship, created in Christ Jesus for good*
> *works, which God prepared ahead of time for us to do.*

EPHESIANS 2:10

While God's work does not depend on us, our work does depend on Him. He has given us good work to do, and we must pursue it in order to find fulfillment.

The idea of pursuing our God-given work—not simply enduring it—can be hard to understand in a culture that views work as both a means of survival and capital gains. One of my favorite Christian thinkers, Dorothy L. Sayers tackles this dilemma in her 1942 essay entitled, "Why Work?" In it, she argues for a distinctly Christian vision of calling and vocation that receives work as a good gift in itself. "Work is the natural exercise and function of man[kind] – the creature who is made in the image of his Creator," she writes. "It is the full expression of the worker's faculties, the thing in which he finds spiritual, mental and bodily satisfaction, and the medium in which he offers himself to God."[9]

For me, perceiving my own work as an offering back to God has changed everything about how I engage in it. Whether it's the work of typing words into a document, cooking dinner for my family, or cleaning out my inbox, I find significant fulfillment in knowing that even the most mundane tasks are not meaningless because they come from Him. In tackling them, I am returning myself back to Him in small, ordinary ways. Of course, this attitude doesn't mean people should take advantage of our work. It's not an invitation for employers or ministries to abuse the relationship with workers and staff. Indeed, the exact opposite is true. Understanding that everyone's work comes from God, means honoring it all the more.

☀ God's Logic

Despite Ecclesiastes's often pessimistic and confusing tone, it resonates deeply with the rest of Scripture. For example, we've seen how the Teacher's observations name the brokenness of a cursed world; we've also seen how his questions align with those that Jesus himself answered. Here in Ecclesiastes 3, we find another connection. The categories the Teacher uses to describe God's plan for human work closely parallel the categories that Paul uses in Ephesians 2:8-10 to explain God's plan for our salvation. Among other things, these parallels suggest that God acts out of a deep, coherent logic that pervades all of creation.

☀ *Compare Paul's Words to Those of the Teacher*

	ECCLESIASTES 3:9-15	EPHESIANS 2:8-10
GOD HAS WORK FOR HUMANS	"the task that God has given the children of Adam to keep them occupied"	"good works which God prepared ahead of time for us to do"
GOD'S WORK DOES NOT DEPEND ON US	"there is no adding to it or taking from it"	"this is not from yourselves; it is God's gift—not from works"
FOR HIS GLORY	"so that people will be in awe of him"	"so that no one can boast"

To find joy in our work under the sun, we must confess that our work, regardless of quality or kind, is not enough to preserve and sustain us. Not only can we not control outcomes, even our successes (our "good works") are not enough to keep us safe—in this life or the next. For this, we must trust God and His work, accepting that all is grace. All goodness, success, abundance that we receive comes from the hand of the Father who is working in and through us.

REREAD ECCLESIASTES 3:15 IN THE CSB VERSION.

Whatever is, has already been, and whatever will be, already is. However; God seeks justice for the persecuted.

According to the Teacher, what is one of the primary works God is doing in the world?

Does the Teacher's focus on justice here surprise you? Why or why not?

What might justice have to do with trusting God's work and not your own?

Another challenge to working in a broken world is that, if we're not careful, it can become a kind of coping mechanism against *hevel*. We work and work and work trying to protect ourselves from harm in an unjust world. However, sometimes work itself becomes a vehicle of injustice, as we oppress each other through wage theft, enslavement, workplace harassment, and piracy. In such a world, it is almost impossible to simply enjoy the work God has given us to do, unless we know that God is working on our behalf. Unless we know that God Himself is seeking "justice for the persecuted."

When we know that God is pursuing justice and that His work will be accomplished, we can rest. In fact, God's work of justice was best displayed with Jesus's work on the cross—providing justification for all who are oppressed by the weight of sin. And suddenly, we come full circle.

God is at work, reconciling and restoring the world through His grace. You can trust that His plans will be accomplished. You can rest in the justification that comes through Christ Jesus; and thus resting, enjoy whatever good work He has given you to do.

Think About It

How do you navigate the tension between overestimating what your work can accomplish and not giving up entirely? Do you swing from extremes, having spurts of ambition in one season, and simply surviving the next? If so, how can you find a steady rhythm of work and expectation? If not, how can you maintain that balance?

WORKING IN LIGHT OF ETERNITY

Just as he did when he explored the limits of pleasure and knowledge, the Teacher runs up against the reality of death while considering work under the sun. How does the brevity of life affect our understanding of the work we do? How does knowing we'll one day die change how we live?

READ ECCLESIASTES 9:7-10.

In verse 7, the Teacher encourages us to enjoy life because "God has already accepted your works." Based on what you know about the relationship between human work and God's work, what do you think this phrase means and doesn't mean?

How does knowing that God has already "accepted your works" free you to enjoy the reward of your labors ("bread" and "wine") with a cheerful heart instead of an anxious one?

Another reason we should enjoy our work is because our days are "fleeting" (vv. 9-10). How does the brevity of life lead us to receive it with joy and gratitude?

After encouraging us to enjoy life, the Teachers seemed to change gears, telling us to work diligently at whatever we're doing. According to verse 10, why is the shortness of life a reason to work hard?

Because our days are short, they should be filled with both joy and hard work, both celebration and diligence. With these paradoxical truths, the Teacher captured the wisdom of working in light of eternity: You will one day die so pay attention to how you use the time you've been given.

GOSPEL TRUTH

Interestingly, Jesus also teaches His disciples to pay attention to how they use their time, urging them to be busy about the work of God. While healing a blind man, He said,

> *This came about so that God's works might be displayed in him. We must do the works of him who sent me while it is day. Night is coming when no one can work.*

> *JOHN 9:3b-4*

And in Ephesians 5, Paul wrote,

> *Pay careful attention, then, to how you walk—not as unwise people but as wise—making the most of the time, because the days are evil. So don't be foolish, but understand what the Lord's will is.*

> *EPHESIANS 5:15-17*

In both passages, the logic is the same as the Teacher's: The time is short. The moment is now. Be busy doing the work God has given you.

But this brings up important questions: *How will we know if we've done enough? How will we know if we've sufficiently "made the most of the time"? How will we know if we've worked "with all our might"?*

After all, we can always push ourselves just one more mile. We can always stay up just a little bit later. We can take on one more project. Is that what they mean by YOLO and *carpe diem*? Is that what it means to make the most of your time?

Think About It

How do you determine when you've done enough and you can rest? Do you ever feel guilty for stopping before a job is finished? Explain.

Working in light of eternity means working for those things that will last, working for those things that have weight and glory.

To understand what it means to work in light of eternity, we must remember a few things. First, working in light of eternity does not mean working for God's acceptance or trying to prove your worth. God has already "accepted your works." And even though He has ordained good works for you (Eph. 2:10), those works do not keep you safe or make you righteous.

Second, working in light of eternity does not necessarily mean cramming as many things into life as possible. It does not mean filling up your days because you're afraid you'll miss out on something. Instead, working in light of eternity means working for those things that will last, working for those things that have weight and glory.

Learning the difference between temporal and eternal things can be hard when everything feels weighty. This is especially true in seasons of life filled with mundane work, like caring for young children or an aging loved one. But when I think of someone who worked in light of eternity, I think of my maternal grandmother, Stella.

She was the hardest working woman I've ever known. If you showed up at her small whitewashed house, you might find her mowing the grass, hanging out laundry, canning grapes, foraging in the woods, or maybe caring for one of her grandchildren. But there was more to it for her than simply being a hard worker.

On a small plaque that hung in her living room were these simple words:

"Only one life, 'twill soon be past,

Only what's done for Christ will last."[10]

Even as a small child I knew these words were being lived out in front of me. Somehow I knew that my grandmother's care and hard work was motivated by a deeper vision of things.

Years later, I learned that the words on that plaque came from a longer poem by Charles T. Studd, who became famous for mission work. Believing that his "one life" was best used in vocational ministry, he left a privileged background in England to sail to China in 1885. Biographies and films commemorate his sacrifice and legacy.

Compared to C. T. Studd, my grandmother's life might seem small and inconsequential. After all, she never went on mission or did anything that made her famous. But in God's eyes, the "what" of her work wasn't as important as the "why" and "how." As the poem says, "what's done for Christ will last." Faithfully serving those under her care, my grandmother taught me that working for eternity need not mean having a grand or dramatic life. It simply means loving God by loving and serving the souls entrusted to us.

READ 1 CORINTHIANS 3:5-15.

In this passage, Paul reiterated many of the truths we've learned about work from Ecclesiastes. Review verses 5-9 and note where each principle shows up:

1. God assigns our work. _____

2. We receive reward for our labor. _____

3. We are working in partnership with God. _____

Next, Paul addressed the quality of the work we do, calling us to pursue work that will last. Review verses 10-15 and answer the questions below.

According to verses 10-11, what is the only foundation stable enough to support our life's work?

List the materials Paul named in verse 12 that could be used to "build" on that foundation.

Which of the materials listed in verse 13 will pass through the fire and survive?

Summarize the core idea of this passage and consider what materials you're building with.

Again, when we talk about working in light of eternity, we don't mean working as hard as possible or just trying to get a lot of things done. We don't even mean only doing "spiritual" activities like prayer, Bible reading, or attending church (even though these are good and necessary practices). Instead, we're talking about investing in things that will stand the test of time—things that will last because they are built on the foundation of Jesus Christ and done in God's name.

A few chapters later in 1 Corinthians 10:31, Paul revisited this idea, showing that the why and who of our work is more important than the what:

> So, whether you eat or drink, or whatever you do,
> do everything for the glory of God.

1 CORINTHIANS 10:31

Ultimately, knowing we have limited time on this earth both frees us to enjoy the time God has given us while also motivating us to make the best use of it. When we center God in our work and entrust it to Him, we will find ourselves working in light of eternity.

WORKING IN WISDOM

Remember that Ecclesiastes presents a true account of life "under the sun." It records in brutal honesty the struggles and challenges of work. But the Teacher doesn't leave us hopeless. In this final section, he will encourage us to continue taking risks in our work and commit ourselves to it even though—and even because—we can't control outcomes.

READ ECCLESIASTES 11:1-6.

What illustration does the Teacher use to describe investing in and cultivating our work (vv. 4,6)?

What are some things mentioned in this passage that are outside the farmer's control that could affect the success of his crop?

Despite these uncertainties, the Teacher seems optimistic in a way he hasn't been previously, encouraging the readers to work hard at the task God has given them. What do you think changed?

In verse 5, the Teacher says "you don't know the work of God who makes everything." How does not knowing what God intends an encouragement to work despite the possibility of loss?

The Teacher's reasoning at this point is remarkable. Not knowing how God will work keeps us working. While uncertainty could mean hardship, it could just as easily mean blessing. As we learn to trust God's unseen hand—and not our own effort—we can work with confidence, even when the outcome is unclear.

☀ Difficult Passage

Ecclesiastes 11:1 is one of the more oblique texts in the book. It advises us to "Send your bread on the surface of the water, for after many days you may find it." This is a good example of why a direct, literal reading of the text cannot always reveal its meaning. While we don't know exactly what the Teacher meant, he is undoubtedly not advising us to go down to the lake and throw Wonder Bread® on the water. So what could this statement mean?

Scholars think this is likely a commonly known saying or parable whose meaning has been lost to time. Some ancient traditions understand it to be a call to charity or generosity and indeed, an ancient proverb from "The Instructions of Onkhsheshonqy" sounds very similar: "Do good, throw your bread on the waters, and one day you will be rewarded" (19:10).[11] But it seems most scholars highlight the contextual association with business and work and see this proverb as encouraging a level of risk-taking despite the uncertainty of the future. Regardless of the exact meaning, the larger implication is clear: There are times in life when we must act in faith before knowing exactly how things will turn out. In this way, measured risk—whether it relates to charity or business—is an invitation to trust God's overarching providence and purpose.

A SEED IN THE GROUND

Toward the end of His earthly ministry, Jesus described His coming death as seed planted in the ground:

> *The hour has come for the Son of Man to be glorified. Truly*
> *I tell you, unless a grain of wheat falls to the ground and dies,*
> *it remains by itself. But if it dies, it produces much fruit.*

JOHN 12:23-24

I wonder what the disciples thought when they heard this? Following Jesus's predictions of His death and resurrection in Matthew, Mark, and Luke, the disciples were confused, perplexed. Perhaps they thought this couldn't be how it was supposed to end. Surely Jesus would be lifted up, come into His earthly kingdom, and bring them with Him. After all they'd sacrificed, was it really going to end in death?

But just as the Teacher testifies in Ecclesiastes: We don't know the work of God. And because we don't, we should plant our seed anyway.

So that's exactly what Jesus lived and modeled for us in His perfect obedience to the Father. Trusting that God would work in ways none of us could imagine, He planted the seed of His life. Knowing that fruit would come from this sacrifice, He surrendered Himself to death. He died knowing that God would be faithful. And three days later, the Seed that had been crushed and planted in the ground, broke forth in new life.

Just as God promised it would.

UNEXPECTEDLY GOOD NEWS

In 1 Corinthians 15:54-57, Paul reminded us of the hope found in the resurrection:

> *Death has been swallowed up in victory.*
> *Where, death, is your victory?*
> *Where, death, is your sting?*
> *The sting of death is sin, and the power of sin is the law. But thanks*
> *be to God, who gives us the victory though our Lord Jesus Christ!*

1 CORINTHIANS 15:54-57

But then, Paul continued in a completely unexpected way.

Read and write out 1 Corinthians 15:58.

Don't miss that last phrase: "Your labor in the Lord is not in vain." Do you see what Paul was saying? Do you see the connection to Ecclesiastes?

This whole time, the Teacher has been searching for the answer to this question: Does my work matter? What is the point of all man's labors? Is it worth it? Or is my work in vain? And here, in 1 Corinthians 15, we finally get the answer.

READ 1 CORINTHIANS 15:58 AGAIN.

What does "therefore" refer to?

On what basis did Paul say that our labor in the Lord is not in vain?

We can
continue in
our work
with joy and
expectation
. . . because
we've
entrusted our
work to God.

If anyone could be tempted to think His work was meaningless, if anyone could be tempted to wonder whether His sacrifice was in vain, if anyone could be tempted to think that God had forgotten Him, it was Jesus. But if anyone could show what true wisdom and faithful obedience looked like, it was also Jesus. Like a grain of wheat, He laid His body into the ground, trusting that the Father would raise Him up again and bring life to the world.

So too, when we're tempted to despair, to think that our work doesn't matter or that God has overlooked it, all we must do is remember the resurrection. God has already proven His faithfulness. He has already proven that He works behind the scenes in unexpected ways. He has already proven that He does not overlook our labor.

So too, it is only when the Teacher understands the limits of his work under the sun that he can rest in God's faithfulness instead of his own. In the way, Ecclesiastes yet again reshapes and reframes our questions, delivering us to exactly the point we need to be to receive God's grace. With Paul and with the Teacher, we can continue in our work with joy and expectation—not because there won't be disappointments or setbacks along the way—but because we've entrusted our work to God.

REFLECTION

Session 5

*Below you'll find some questions to help you think through
and apply what you've learned in this week of study.
Be prepared to discuss these if you're doing the study in a group.*

1   **Which day of study this week was your favorite and why?**

2   **How would you summarize the Teacher's view of working under the sun?**

3   **How does this compare to what Jesus and the New Testament writers taught about working under the sun?**

4   **What are the main takeaways for you from this week and how do they apply to your life?**

*If you're leading a group, check out the leader guide
found at lifeway.com/lifeunderthesun.*

COMMUNITY UNDER THE SUN

Throughout the book of Ecclesiastes, the Teacher explored life in the context of community. While he speaks from a personal perspective, he assumes relationships with other people. But these relationships were not always healthy and often, a source of pain and frustration. Is this all we can expect from our relationships with each other here on earth? Or can we learn to accept the reality of difficult relationships while also cultivating good ones?

WORKING TOGETHER

The Teacher begins his consideration of human relationships in a slightly unexpected place: our work.

READ ECCLESIASTES 4:4-8.

According to the Teacher in verse 4, what negative motive drives human ambition and work?

What family relationships does the Teacher mention in verse 8? Why do you think he mentions family relationships in context of work?

What question does the person who is alone in the world ask about his struggles?

Compare the motivation for work in verse 4 with the motivation for work in verse 8. What is the difference?

From the beginning, communal life looms large in Ecclesiastes, even if it is somewhat assumed. Chapter 1 wonders about the generations who have gone before and whether anyone will remember us after we're gone (1:11). In chapter 2, the Teacher speaks of using other people for his own pleasure (2:7-8) and comments on his professional rivals (2:21). By chapter 3, he is pondering the collective fate of humanity (3:19). But in many ways, the Teacher seems to relate to people as objects or characters in his personal story. Here in chapter 4, however, he finally begins to consider the significance of relationships and the need for companions on life's journey. Interestingly enough, he begins by considering them through the lens of work.

Last week we learned that even before the fall, God gave human beings meaningful work to do. And now, though work is a struggle under the sun, it also holds the potential for reward and fulfillment. Work also has potential to create deep partnerships and supports our relationships with each other. As he often does, the Teacher highlights this reality by negation. He observes a person who doesn't have a companion with which to share his work and how that affected his ability to continue to struggle against the challenges of life. What's the point of doing all this, of sacrificing and striving, if you don't have someone to work for and with? What's the point if you come to the end of your life and all you have to show for your work is money?

Think About It

Who are the people in your life that inspire your work? Who are your partners in your work? How do these relationships inspire you to do your best work?

SHARED WORK

It's significant that the Teacher names family relationships ("brother" and "son") in his observation about work and human community because we see this same category early in Genesis. In the ancient world, family and work were more closely aligned that they are in our contemporary culture. While we still know people who have a "family business," this distinction was a moot point in the ancient world. A household was both family and business. Generational wealth passed down through blood lines. But rather than inheriting money, children often inherited land, livestock, and specific professional skills. So, it makes sense that the Teacher was thinking in context of familial relationships when he considered who would inherit his work.

But there's more going on in this passage beyond individual families, something about how work can create community. Last week we considered the creation mandate in Genesis 1:27-28, that moment when God tasked the first humans to steward the earth:

> *God blessed them, and God said to them, "Be fruitful, multiply,*
> *fill the earth, and subdue it. Rule the fish of the sea, the birds*
> *of the sky, and every creature that crawls on the earth."*

> *GENESIS 1:28*

We stated that the mandate is not two commands, it's one. Here's how it works: as the man and woman venture out into the world, they create community by bringing other image bearers into existence. This community then works together to "subdue the earth." The two threads of relationship and work wrap around each other. Our work benefits one another; and in turn, these partnerships enable us to work more effectively. Just as the Teacher observed, our work is fueled and stabilized by our relationships with other people.

This understanding of community is deeply at odds with our individualistic culture. For us, personal relationships are private while our work is seen as a path to self-actualization and/or wealth creation. (The Teacher hints at this kind of thinking in Ecclesiastes 4:4 when he suggests that jealousy drives a lot of human activity.) But both Genesis and Ecclesiastes offer us a vision of shared life and shared work. At the end of the day, negative desires like greed, avarice, and envy are not generative. They cannot create. They can only compete. Meanwhile, work that emerges from love of others and the desire to provide for them has the potential to be deeply imaginative and life-giving. It also has the potential to bind us together in community.

Think About It

Do you have any close relationships that began with a shared project? How does working together have the potential to form bonds and create community?

WORK IN THE FAMILY OF GOD

In Matthew 28, Jesus sends his followers into the world, telling them,

Go, therefore, and make disciples of all nations, baptizing them in the name of the Father, the Son and of the Holy Spirit, teaching them to observe everything I have commanded you.

MATTHEW 28:19-20a

In many ways, this "Great Commission" parallels the creation mandate of Genesis 1: those who bear the likeness of Christ are sent into the world to birth others ("make disciples") who will also bear His likeness. Working together, they will create a community of blessing and goodness—the church—that stewards the gifts of God, while longing, praying, and working to see His will done on earth as it is in heaven.

And just as God intended from the beginning, working together for His kingdom binds us in union and communion. As we work together for something larger than any one of us, this shared sense of purpose creates relationships with people we might never have known otherwise. As we bring our separate gifts and capacities to the work, we find ourselves increasingly dependent on each other. As we learn the value of each member of the community, we learn that their contributions are just as important as our own. We learn that we need them as much as they need us.

If you've ever played in a band or orchestra, you probably have a sense of what I'm describing here. Or perhaps, like me, you grew up singing in school and church choirs, learning what it means to carry your particular part and work together in harmony. Somehow, even though they're each singing a particular note, the soprano, alto, tenor, and bass sections blend into one remarkable sound. In fact, Jeremy Begbie, a theologian whose specializes in the intersection of art and theology, suggests that a musical chord represents God's vision for union and communion.[12] Each individual note retains its unique properties but somehow, when combined, they create an entirely distinct sound.

> Just as God intended from the beginning, working together for His kingdom binds us in union and communion.

It's almost as if mutual dependence were built into creation from the beginning. It's almost as if God made the world for community.

Understanding the significance of our common life together is key to understanding God's work in the world. It's key to understanding why we're called to love our neighbors as we love ourselves. We are created for relationship with each other, to live bonded together, sharing our joys, our sorrows, and our work under the sun.

SHARING LIFE, SHARING SUFFERING

As the text unfolds, the Teacher continues to explore why human companionship is so important to life under the sun—not despite the futility we encounter but precisely because of it.

READ ECCLESIASTES 4:9-12.

According to verse 9, why are two better than one?

In verses 10-12, list how two is better than one in each case:

Verse 10

Verse 11

Verse 12

This section opens by stating the positive affect of companionship: Two people working together will be more productive and potentially achieve a better reward or outcome than one person working alone. This practical reality is predicated on a deeper one: Human beings are designed to need other human beings.

Yesterday, we considered how Genesis 1:27-28 suggests that working together helps form the bonds of human community. But looking closer at the text, we realize the connection between work and community rests on the fact that human identity is inherently communal.

REREAD GENESIS 1:27 BELOW.

So God created man[kind]
in his own image;
he created him in the image of God;
he created them male and female.

Notice the plural pronoun in verse 27 that is repeated in verse 28. Notice as well the image of God is manifested collectively as male and female. It's no surprise, then, that when we read the Genesis 2 creation account God says, "It is not good for the man to be alone. I will make a helper corresponding to him" (Gen. 2:18).

But instead of immediately making the woman, God paraded the animals in front of the man to see what the man would name them. During this process, it became clear that no animal would be a suitable companion—none was "corresponding to him" (Gen. 2:20). None of the animals were human like he was human.

So God put the man to sleep, took one of the man's ribs and created woman. He created her this way so that despite her differences, she would still be of the same substance as he is—human. When the man woke up, that sameness was the first thing he recognized about the woman. "This one, at last, is bone of my bone and flesh of my flesh," he said (2:23a). He had finally found a human companion—who though different from him, was fundamentally suited to him because of their shared humanity.

Think About It

How does human companionship differ from animal companionship? What does each provide that the other cannot?

SHARED SUFFERING

Returning to Ecclesiastes 4:9-12, we notice a change in the Teacher's tone between verses 9 and 10. While he begins by focusing solely on the positive reward of human companionship in verse 9, he quickly shifts to a negative posture to accentuate the reward. He names danger after danger that puts a single person in peril. A fall. The cold. Physical attack. The message is clear: Human companionship is more than a blessing to life under the sun. It is a necessity.

This shift in Ecclesiastes 4 mirrors a shift in Genesis, both in its severity and speed. No sooner did the first man and woman find each other in blessed companionship than the world was thrown into chaos through the Fall. By Genesis 3, their relationship was marred by strife and conflict. By Genesis 4, Cain had killed Abel. The *hevel* of the world was undeniable and had momentum.

But despite the *hevel*—or perhaps because of it—we must find trustworthy companions who will journey with us through our days under the sun. Like Ruth and Naomi, we need companions whose faithfulness is forged in the crucible of shared suffering. We need the deep trust and commitment that can say,

For wherever you go, I will go,
and wherever you live, I will live;
your people will be my people,
and your God will be my God.
Where you die, I will die,
and there I will be buried.
May the Lord punish me,
and do so severely,
if anything but death separates you and me.

RUTH 1:16b-17

Think About It

Do you have a friend or family member you can count on to be present with you in trials and suffering? If so, who is it and why that person? How meaningful is it to know this person would show up for you?

☀ A Cord of Three Strands

Despite being one of the most often quoted sections of Ecclesiastes, this proverb is something of a curiosity. The motif of the "three-fold cord" was not unknown in the ancient world and shows up in other ancient literature but the poetic structure of Ecclesiastes plays with the phrase in unique ways.

For example, consider how the author moves from comparing *two* and *one* only to conclude the section with a final flourish of *three*. This technique is common in Hebrew poetry and is known as numerical parallelism. (See example of this structure in Prov. 6:16.)

The goal of numerical parallelism is to use the readers' understanding of mathematics to intensify a phrase and propel it forward. By counting upward, the poet activates the reader's mind so that they naturally take the next logical step. If the Lord hates six things, then how must He feel about seven? And here, if two is better than one, then what does that suggest about three? Because we already know the goodness of *two*, we naturally assume that *three* must be even better.

Throughout church history, interpreters have also seen hidden meaning in the numerology of *three*. Some assigned Christological significance saying that when Jesus is the center of a human relationship, like a marriage, it will be unbreakable. Others see Trinitarian allusions, with the "three-strand cord" referring to Father, Son, and Holy Spirit. Still others name the cords as the virtues of faith, hope, and love. Such speculations and applications aren't necessarily inconsistent with the text, but the Teacher himself only had a basic principle in mind: Human relationship can be a source of strength and defense in a dangerous world.

THE LAW OF CHRIST

This vision of sharing suffering is not limited to Ecclesiastes or the Old Testament. In fact, the gospel assumes that following in the way of Jesus will compel us to journey together through both physical and spiritual dangers. In Galatians 6:1, for example, the apostle Paul called believers to lift up those who are "overtaken in any wrongdoing . . ." in order to restore them. He also implored us to "Carry one another's burdens; in this way you will fulfill the law of Christ" (Gal. 6:1-2).

While the Teacher likely did not have spiritual restoration or encouragement in view in Ecclesiastes 4, the principle is the same. In a dangerous world, we need each other. We need each other when we fall, when we triumph, when we're under spiritual attack, and when we're suffering.

In so doing, we reflect the One who came to us in our suffering—who Himself became a friend to sinners and cared for us. In this way, we learn to fulfill the law of Christ and love our neighbor as we love ourselves.

A GOOD NAME

Having emphasized the need for companionship, the Teacher turns to consider the dynamics of life together, including who and what we elevate in our communities.

READ ECCLESIASTES 7:1.

What do you think "name" refers to in verse 1?

Why would the Teacher use the image of "fine perfume" to refer to a person's reputation or public character?

Verse 1 shifts from a generally positive image to a negative one. What feelings does this shift evoke for you as a reader?

The language and categories of Ecclesiastes 7:1 may sound familiar. Consider the following parallel passages:

A good name is to be chosen over great wealth;
favor is better than silver and gold.

PROVERBS 22:1

Dead flies make a perfumer's oil ferment and stink; so
a little folly outweighs wisdom and honor.

ECCLESIASTES 10:1

Together, these verses convey the importance of our character and how easily trust can be lost to foolishness. But these verses also raise interesting questions about the relationship between community, reputation, and public perception. Unfortunately, some conflate a "good name" with celebrity, fame, and influence. Instead of evaluating the strength of "name" on personal character and integrity, weight is given to a person's popularity, social standing, or the number of followers they have on social media.

On a personal level, most of us do not face the temptation of fame to establish a "good name." However, within our own communities, we might be tempted to chose popularity and being "liked" over personal integrity. We might choose to present a false front or craft a certain image to be accepted or gain influence. This kind of "image crafting" is particularly enticing in the digital age that allows us to curate what others see of our lives and choices.

Think About It

What are the differences between being famous, having a good reputation, and cultivating personal integrity? Who is a person in your life, living or dead, you would describe as having a "good name"? What marks their character?

CONTINUE BY READING ECCLESIASTES 7:1-4.

What surprising statement does the Teacher make in the second half of verse 1?

List why the Teacher lifts up the house of mourning and grief over the house of feasting or pleasure. Then, explain his reasoning in your own words.

What words or phrases allude to suffering in Ecclesiastes 7:1-4?

By now, you know that Ecclesiastes is an unpredictable book. Just when you think it's going in one direction, it breaks toward another. In this passage, the Teacher begins by reminding us of the importance of a good name, but then plunged headlong into death, suffering, and grief. What's the connection?

At the very least, the Teacher sees a link between facing death and cultivating character in community. There's something about considering "the end of all mankind" (7:2) that can help us take stock of our lives and seek to become people who have a "good name." But verse 3 presses the point even further. Grief can have a formative effect on our character. And this, perhaps more than anything, flies in the face of the way we tend to understand influence, fame, and celebrity.

Think about the modern phenomenon of the "Influencer" or a person who has the ability to affect a community's choices. It might be a famous politician, a sports star, or a Hollywood A-lister. But it could just as easily be someone on social media with millions of followers who is "famous for being famous."

Perhaps one reason influencers have power in the first place is because we believe they have somehow escaped suffering and grief. They look like they have it all together—wealthy, beautiful, well-adjusted, successful, loved, and adored by their family. And because we want to believe that we, too, could be so #blessed and bypass suffering, we follow them. We want what we think they have.

But if the Teacher is correct, one path to maturity is the way of suffering. And a "good name" is best cultivated by facing grief and death head on, not by projecting false narratives about happiness and success. Suffering is an ever-present companion in life under the sun. So instead of denying it, we should let it shape our character, mold us into people who value deeper things, and allow it to transform us and make us people truly worthy of a "good name."

When you think of the specific griefs in your own life, you might think of "before" and "after"—especially if it was a traumatic event like a house fire, an unwanted divorce, or the death of a child. You feel like you can't quite reach the person you were "before" and so the loss is greater than the grief itself. You mourn the life you had as well as what might have been. Metaphysical poet John Donne (1572–1631) explored these themes of love, loss, and suffering in works that includes the now famous lines "no man is an island;" "for whom the bell tolls;" and "death be not proud." Much of Donne's work emerged from his own suffering, including a brief imprisonment, the deaths of his children, and the loss of his beloved wife Anne after sixteen years of marriage. In a brief devotional meditation, he described the work of grief in his own life this way: "No man hath affliction [sic] enough, that is not matured and ripened by it, and made fit for God by that affliction."[13] For Donne, suffering and grief were unavoidable, but meaning was not. Entrusted to God, suffering could mature and prepare us for a more intimate relationship with Him.

Think About It

How has grief and loss formed you? How has it shaped your character? How has it enabled others to entrust you with their griefs and form meaningful relationships?

IN HER MEMORY

READ MATTHEW 26:6-13.

What is the setting of this story? Why are they gathered there?

Who is the guest of honor? Who has a good reputation?

List any commonalities that you see between this story and Ecclesiastes 7:1-4.

The anointing of Jesus's feet is also recorded in Mark 14 and John 12; and while each author highlights different details, the core story is the same. Jesus is feasting with His disciples and friends when a woman comes with fine perfume to anoint Him. She is focused, unconcerned by the gaze of others, and breaking open the vial, pours the oil on Him. When the disciples object to her lavish display of affection and praise, Jesus rebukes them, saying that she is preparing his body for suffering, death, and burial.

Read through the lens of Ecclesiastes 7:1-4, the parallels are unmistakable. While sitting in the house of feasting, Jesus speaks of the house of mourning. And among those who thought they had a "good name," a humble woman is wiser than them all. Jesus receives her worship and blesses her. In the community He is creating, she will be remembered. She will have a good name and be known for loving and honoring the One whose name is above every other.

Think About It

In what ways might pursuing earthly approval keep you from falling at Jesus's feet in authentic worship? What can you do to cultivate communities that honor this kind of authenticity?

AUTHORITY UNDER THE SUN (PART 1)

Living in community requires order, boundaries, and governance, but these structures can very quickly become corrupted. How should we respond to leaders who take advantage of the power entrusted to them?

READ ECCLESIASTES 8:1-5.

Verse 1 describes the physical change that happens when we have insight on a problem that has been troubling us. The moment of wisdom "brightens [the] face." What images or words do we use today to describe this same phenomenon?

On what basis should we "keep the king's command?" What does this imply about who is the higher authority (8:2)?

In verses 3-4, why does the Teacher suggest not challenging the authority of the king directly? What do you think of this advice?

What did the Teacher mean when he said "a wise heart knows the right time and procedure" (8:5)? How has this played out practically in your life?

The Teacher opens chapter 8 stating that sudden awareness "brightens" the face. Cartoonists often capture this moment as a light bulb illuminating above someone's head. But this introduction also reminds us of a harder truth: applying wisdom to relationships often begins with confusion. While proverbs are neat and contained, the problems of life require us to puzzle through them. Wisdom happens in process. Understanding this progressive enlightenment is especially important as we engage with other people—people who are just as complicated and confused as we are. In this passage, for example, the Teacher highlights the difficulty of relating to leaders who are foolish or harmful. *How should you respond as a person under their authority? What kinds of things do you need to take into consideration?*

The Teacher begins by naming reality, noting the relationship between the king's authority and God's authority. While he advises us to "keep the king's command," the reason for the advice is perhaps more important. We relate to community leaders a certain way because our primary allegiance is to God, not to the leaders themselves. This suggests a couple of things. First, the leader is not divine or inherently better than us. And second, human leaders can be wrong.

If you've lived any length of time, you've probably been disappointed by a leader—parent, teacher, pastor, or some other leader. But the experience of being disappointed didn't prepare you to know how to deal with it or how to think rightly about human leadership. Some people, for example, will minimize or deny a leader's flaws to maintain their own equilibrium. Others might reject human authority altogether to protect themselves from future disappointment.

But the Teacher takes a different approach. He counsels careful discernment instead of unquestioning obedience. He knows community leaders are human with a tendency to make mistakes and misuse their power. Part of that careful discernment means understanding your own relative power in relationship to them.

You can pray and hope that leaders use their power well, but at the end of the day, the nature of authority means they will do what they want. In response, the Teacher counsels us to navigate our circumstances with both subtlety and humility, being aware of what we can and cannot accomplish. All the while entrusting ourselves to God.

Think About It

When did you first become aware that leaders, like your parents, your pastor, or your civic rulers were fallible? How did that affect the way you viewed them? Followed their leadership?

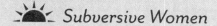 ## Subversive Women

In the ancient world, male heads of household held authority over the women, children, and servants. Unlike our modern context that presumes individual rights, relational dynamics at the time of Ecclesiastes were much more communal, locking individuals into imbalanced relationships. This difference in social arrangement helps explain biblical stories in which women and servants act in seemingly furtive ways. Such stories do not teach we can do wrong in order to do right, but that people with limited power cannot act in the same ways that those with power can. Instead, doing good while in a position of limited power might mean acting subversively, by either undermining or passively resisting. It would be easy for modern readers to interpret subversion as a lack of integrity, but the Scripture doesn't use this metric. Instead it seems to judge a lack of directness by the goal of such action: *Are those without power subverting oppression or are they subverting goodness? Are they resisting evil in the ways they can or are they benefiting from it?* Compare and contrast the following characters. Each one used indirect means to accomplish certain goals while having vastly different motivations.

JUDGED RIGHTEOUS	JUDGED UNRIGHTEOUS
Jochebed and Hebrew midwives undermined a plot to kill innocents *(Ex. 1:15-2:10)*	Potiphar's wife plotted against the innocent *(Gen. 39:1-20)*
Abigail subverted her husband's foolishness *(1 Sam. 25:2-42)"*	Jezebel enabled her husband's foolishness *(1 Kings 21:1-16)*
Esther risked power and privilege on behalf of others *(Esth. 4:8–5:8)*	Zeresh (Haman's wife) sought power and privilege at cost of others *(Esth. 5:9-14)*
Jael was instrumental in the death of an enemy of Israel *(Judg. 4:17-21)*	Herodias was instrumental in the death of a prophet of Israel *(Mark 6:14-29)*

WISE AS SERPENTS, HARMLESS AS DOVES

READ MATTHEW 10:16-20.

What four animals did Jesus allude to in verse 16? How did He use the natural world to make His point? What does each animal represent?

Verse 17 moves us from the natural world to human civilization. What did Jesus warn them would happen?

What help would they receive and from whom (vv. 19-20)?

When Jesus sent His disciples out to preach the gospel, He instructed them on how to relate to community leaders. He anticipated His followers would be handed over to civic rulers who would demand answers from them. It's in this context that Jesus offered the famous command to be "wise as serpents and harmless as doves" (KJV).

This axiom captures the important tension of being aware of the brokenness of the world while not contributing to it. We much anticipate that the *hevel* of life extends to human community and human leadership while not becoming complicit with it ourselves. But there's something more happening here. Both the Teacher and Jesus agree on the importance of navigating abusive leadership with wisdom and grace. But Jesus noted something that the Teacher did not: The wisdom we need to engage community leaders will come from a divine source.

In Matthew 10:19-20, Jesus told His followers to not worry about what or how they should respond when questioned. Instead of letting their fear dominate them (or make their faces "stern" in the words of Eccl. 8:1), they should rest in the promise that the Spirit would give them insight how and when they needed it. They should rest in the promise that the Spirit will bring the "Aha!" moment and that the light bulb will go off just when it's needed.

So while we prepare ourselves for the inevitability of facing flawed leaders, Jesus promises we will not face them alone, nor be left to our own wisdom and ingenuity. Instead, we entrust ourselves to God and allow the Spirit to guide us, making us both wise and harmless.

Think About It

When have you experienced a moment of insight or practical wisdom that seemed to pop into your head from nowhere? What do you attribute that to? How have you experienced the Spirit guiding you through challenging relationships with community leaders and those opposed to the faith in the past?

AUTHORITY UNDER THE SUN (PART 2)

READ ECCLESIASTES 10:4-7.

Why should you not leave your post when a leader is angry at you? Why does this response make practical sense?

What error or mistake does the Teacher note in verse 6? According to verse 5, who is responsible for this kind of mistake?

What is the danger of appointing a fool to a place of great power? Who bears the brunt of this kind of decision?

You might notice that Ecclesiastes 10:4 closely parallels Proverbs 15:1: "A gentle answer turns away anger, but a harsh word stirs up wrath." This kind of continuity reveals Ecclesiastes to be in conversation with the other wisdom books in the Bible and the canon of Scripture as a whole. These small links become even more important when the Teacher offers advice that seems at odds with other passages—like he does in the next few verses.

Continuing the theme of rulers who make decisions foolishly, the Teacher names a reality that is so basic we might miss it: Power begets power. Leaders assign people to "great heights" and "lowly positions" (v. 6) for their own reasons and purposes. In other words, the game is rigged.

Those of us who live in societies that claim to be meritocracies need to pay close attention to this inequity. Meritocracy says people naturally end up in the social strata to which they belong. In this framework, if you're poor, there must be a reason you're at the bottom of the ladder. Perhaps you don't work hard or make foolish choices. On the other hand, if you are socially powerful, then you must be the wisest, most talented, and most deserving.

But in the Teacher's experience, merit isn't the main thing that determines who has social power. Instead, he sees rulers appointing people to certain positions based on the rulers' interests. He sees foolish people given power while others are excluded. There is a randomness about who ends up in certain positions based on who serves the interests of those already in power.

☀ Difficult Passage

Throughout Ecclesiastes, the Teacher uses social categories that are either unfamiliar to modern readers or seen as unjust. In Ecclesiastes 10:6-7, for example, we find the Teacher contrasting the fool with the rich as well as slaves and princes. This passage should not be read as condoning slavery or offering God-ordained social structures. Instead, it reflects the Teacher's context in which power resided with elites and social movement depended on currying their favor.

Despite this ancient context, we can learn from this passage. "Under the sun," rulers elevated and rewarded whomever they wanted based on their own interests. Part of living well in community means acknowledging this injustice and learning to question how our own structures reflect this reality. *Who do we elevate and why? Are we empowering people of integrity and virtue? Or are those in leadership passing authority only to people who serve the leaders interests?*

Think About It

When did you first encounter a situation where the people in charge were not in that position because they were capable or worthy of it? What was your response and how did you deal with the situation?

The Teacher explains how easily private conversations can spread, warning that a "bird of the sky may carry the message, and a winged creature may report the matter" (Eccl. 10:20). Today, we sometimes describe this act with the phrase "a little bird told me."

What are the characteristics of leaders who are a blessing to their people (v. 17)?

Reading verses 17 and 19 together, what is the difference between good feasting and bad feasting?

Why does the Teacher's use of a leaky, collapsing roof as a metaphor for leaders who neglect their duty make sense (v. 18)? What is the underlying truth?

How does the Teacher illustrate the way private conversations can spread?

After the Teacher's blunt assessment of authority under the sun, he returns to offer advice about how to discern good leadership from bad leadership. His underlying assumption is that those entrusted with authority have a responsibility to cultivate their character and integrity precisely because they are in leadership. By looking closely at the text, we can summarize the characteristics of good leaders this way:

1. Good leaders are mature and self-controlled while bad leaders are immature and self-indulgent (vv. 16-17).

2. Good leaders work hard and anticipate the needs of those under their care while bad leaders are lazy and neglectful (v. 18).

3. Good leaders speak carefully because they understand how fast rumors travel while bad leaders speak carelessly (v. 20).

When I consider the impact a good leader can have on a community, I think of Reverend Bob Childress. Bob was a pastor in the southwest-Virginia mountains who planted several churches and revolutionized the area in the early part of the twentieth century. A native son of the Buffalo Mountain area, Childress grew up surrounded by poverty, violence, illiteracy, and alcoholism. But in his late twenties, he encountered the gospel and was called to ministry. Back then, these mountains were more remote than they are even now. With few roads, fewer bridges, and no jobs, people had little hope. To make things worse, this was the era of Prohibition when moonshining and running liquor down to Roanoke was one of the few ways the people of the Buffalo could make a living. But Childress understood that you can't separate the spiritual and physical needs and so as he preached, he also advocated. He petitioned regional and state governments to invest in the area. He helped establish new forms of employment. He brought schools and infrastructure. But he also helped his neighbors imagine and build their future for themselves. When establishing a new congregation, Childress encouraged them to build their building with native rocks that dotted their lands. Today, nearly a hundred years later, these "stone churches" and the congregations that call them home, stand testament to the role good leadership can have in a community's life—now and for eternity.[14]

Think About It

When you consider good leaders, who comes to mind and why?
What have you learned from them that you can apply in your own areas of influence?

UNEXPECTEDLY GOOD NEWS

The earliest readers of Ecclesiastes would have known the sting of flawed rulers firsthand. The kingdom of Israel enjoyed a level of peace and stability during the monarchies of David and Solomon. But instability ruled when the kingdom divided and both nations were led by a series of sinful, foolish kings. Eventually, outside empires: the Assyrians, Babylonians, Greeks, and Romans all ruled over the land of Israel in turn. By the time of Jesus, the Jewish people had endured centuries of untrustworthy and unfaithful rulers.

Worse, they fought among themselves for whatever power was left. This history gives context to Jesus's teaching about authority in His kingdom.

As His disciples were jockeying for position, he rebuked them saying,

> *You know that the rulers of the Gentiles lord it over them, and those in high positions act as tyrants over them. It must not be like that among you. On the contrary, whoever wants to become great among you must be your servant, and whoever wants to be first among you must be your slave; just as the Son of Man did not come to be served, but to serve, and to give his life as a ransom for many.*
>
> *MATTHEW 20:25-28*

Jesus knows exactly what the Teacher knows: Earthly rulers often wield their authority in arbitrary and unjust ways. But Jesus said that it's to be different for His followers. Those who would be great must become servant of all. They must reflect the virtues the Teacher notes in Ecclesiastes.

But Jesus did more than talk about service. He embodied it.

The night before He was crucified, Jesus knelt down and washed His disciples's feet. When He finished, He said,

> *So if I, your Lord and Teacher, have washed your feet, you also ought to wash one another's feet. For I have given you an example that you also should do just as I have done for you.*
>
> *JOHN 13:14-15*

The way of Jesus is not through power, authority, or coercion, but through sacrificial love. Those who follow Him must lead the same way, giving themselves for the good of others. This is exactly what He did for us.

REFLECTION

Session 6

*Below you'll find some questions to help you think through
and apply what you've learned in this week of study.
Be prepared to discuss these if you're doing the study in a group.*

1   **Which day of study this week was your favorite and why?**

2   **How would you summarize the Teacher's view of community under the sun?**

3   **How does this compare to what Jesus and the New Testament writers taught about community under the sun?**

4   **What are the main takeaways for you from this week and how do they apply to your life?**

*If you're leading a group, check out the leader guide
found at* **lifeway.com/lifeunderthesun**.

Session 7

JUSTICE UNDER
THE SUN

At some point in your growing up years, a well-meaning adult may have tried to comfort you with the statement "life isn't fair." The Teacher made a similar observation about life under the sun, recognizing that it is fundamentally unjust and seems to be governed by the whims of fate rather than any kind of divine ordering. But still, even children realize that life should be fair—that something is wrong with a world where the good are punished and evil is rewarded. So how can we make sense of the injustices around us? How can we find meaning and happiness in this life despite its injustice?

A CROOKED WORLD

Today, we're returning to the idea of *hevel* and the limits of our ability to fix all that is wrong with life under the sun.

READ ECCLESIASTES 1:12-15.

How does the Teacher describe what God has given people to do (v. 13)?

According to the Teacher, what is the result of all that is done under the sun (v. 14)?

What two images does he use in verse 15 to describe the futility of life under the sun?

Although we've already considered this text through the lens of wisdom, we're reconsidering it through the lens of justice. At its heart, Ecclesiastes is wrestling with life in a world that is not as it should be. The "futility" or *hevel* that the Teacher mourns includes natural human limits, but more specifically, our inability to correct the fundamental "not right-ness" of the world. As he says in verse 15, "What is crooked cannot be straightened; what is lacking cannot be counted."

The idea that the world is not as it should be sends us back to Genesis again. Remember the first use of *hevel* occurs in Genesis 4 and is the name of Adam and Eve's second son, Abel. Also remember that the previous chapter in Genesis describes how the world became *hevel* after the Fall:

> The ground is cursed because of you.
> You will eat from it by means of painful labor
> all the days of your life.
> It will produce thorns and thistles for you,
> and you will eat the plants of the field.
> You will eat bread by the sweat of your brow
> until you return to the ground,
> since you were taken from it.
> For you are dust,
> and you will return to dust.

GENESIS 3:17b-19

While it would be easy to read Genesis as a product of ancient history, the text is explaining a metaphysical reality—one that transcends time and defines human existence to this day. It speaks to these questions: *Why does the world not work the way it should? Why does all our effort and labor seem to make no impact? Why does it seem so unfair?*

So pervasive is this sense of not right-ness in our world that the apostle Paul said the earth joins in mourning it with us.

READ ROMANS 8:20-23 BELOW.

> For the creation was subjected to futility—not willingly, but because of him who subjected it—in the hope that the creation itself will also be set free from the bondage to decay into the glorious freedom of God's children. For we know that the whole creation has been groaning together with labor pains until now. Not only that, but we ourselves who have the Spirit as the firstfruits—we also groan within ourselves, eagerly waiting for adoption, the redemption of our bodies.

Notice that Paul used the same language as the Teacher to describe the condition of the earth: subjected to futility.

What other similarities to do you see between this passage and Ecclesiastes?

A vision of the world in a perpetual state of *hevel* stands in stark contrast to our modern sense of progress—that we are moving toward better things. But the reality of this futility explains why ancient injustices continue to rear their ugly heads despite our best attempts to quash them. Why racism, sexual abuse, and the oppression of the poor never seem to go away. Why every generation must withstand these atrocities anew.

So when the Teacher describes life under the sun as *hevel*—and goes on and on, chapter after chapter about it—he is simply voicing the longing we all feel as we wait for the world to be made right.

Think About It

Do you tend to have a generally positive or negative view of life under the sun? Are you generally optimistic or pessimistic about humanity's ability to change for the better? How might your age and life experience affect your posture?

Though we grieve the state of our world, a crooked world holds its own kind of hope because a crooked world hints to the fact that a straight one exists. The fact that we long for life to be other than it is tells us we know it should be something more. The fact that we instinctively know life is not fair confirms we know it should be fair.

In fact, this reasoning is what eventually brought Oxford don and author, C. S. Lewis to faith. Seeing the injustices of the world around him, he had determined that God did not exist and life was senseless. (Some might even say, futile.) But as he considered his own argument,

Lewis began to see a flaw in it. "My argument against God was that the universe seemed so cruel and unjust," he wrote. "But how had I got this idea of just and unjust? A man does not call a line crooked unless he has some idea of a straight line. What was I comparing this universe with when I called it unjust?"[15]

Perhaps the question is not, why is life so unfair, but who can make the crooked ways straight?

GOSPEL HOPE

Isaiah 40 offers a word of comfort to people who are struggling under the weight of a crooked world and their own crookedness in it. Speaking through the prophet Isaiah, God promised One whose coming will shake the very foundations of the earth, whose glory will remake and reform its landscape. One who will make the crooked places straight.

> *Every valley shall be exalted, and every mountain and hill shall be made low: and the crooked shall be made straight, and the rough places plain: And the glory of the LORD shall be revealed, and all flesh shall see it together: for the mouth of the LORD hath spoken it.*

ISAIAH 40:4-5, KJV

The One who first made the earth as it should be is the One who will restore it.

WICKEDNESS IN THE PLACE OF JUDGMENT

Even though life is unfair, we still know it should be, and so we work for justice in the ways we can. But what happens when the places that we count on to establish justice turn out to be just as crooked as everywhere else?

READ ECCLESIASTES 3:16-22.

How does the Teacher initially comfort himself at the thought of injustice in the place of judgment (v. 17)?

According to the Teacher, what might be one possible reason that God allows injustice to persist under the sun (v. 18)?

In what way does the Teacher say humans and animals are alike?

What does the Teacher conclude is the only thing a person can do in the face of earthly injustice and God's delayed judgment (v. 22)?

This dense section of text ties together two lines of thought: the reality of injustice and the certainty of death. First, the Teacher recognizes that even our best attempts to pursue justice can be corrupted. Too often, the innocent are punished, and the guilty set free. Initially, the Teacher took consolation in the fact that God will one day judge the righteous and the wicked, setting all things right. But then he seemed to reconsider. Is this really a certainty?

After all, who actually knows what happens after death (v. 22)? All we know for sure is that we will die just like the animals do.

The Teacher is wrestling with what previous generations have called "the fear of God"—a sober-mindedness that comes when you realize you will give an account for your actions. Even if you don't think there will ever be a reason for human systems to punish you, the fear of God helps you resist the temptation to act unjustly. But where there is no fear of God—when people think death is the end and this life is all that exists—they make decisions the same way animals do: they choose to preserve themselves and pursue their own interests. Even if it means acting unjustly toward other people.

Think About It

What role does the possibility of future judgment and reward play in your choices? Do you think this is a helpful or unhelpful frame for living? What does a healthy fear of God look like?

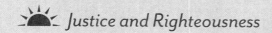 *Justice and Righteousness*

The parallel structure of Ecclesiastes 3:16 offers insight into the link between justice and righteousness. In Scripture, the ideas of righteousness, justice, and judgment are connected in ways not seen in modern usage. The Hebrew word *tsedeq* can be translated as *just, fair,* or *righteous* (*righteousness*) as it is here.[16] Another closely related word *mishpat,* translated in the CSB as judgment refers to a command, decision, ordinance, or decree from an official source.[17] Ideally, such judgments will be just or righteous.[18]

Today, however, we tend to separate justice and righteousness, understanding righteousness in terms of personal piety and justice in terms of public policy. But because the Bible ties justice tightly to God's righteousness, it expects God's people to reflect His character in both their personal dealings and their communities. In fact, the presence of injustice—whether personal or communal—is understood as a form of unrighteousness that must be repented of and purged.

CONTINUE IN THE TEXT BY READING ECCLESIASTES 4:1-3.

The oppressed caught the Teacher's attention. What was the reason for their tears and why did no one comfort them?

Who did the Teacher say are better off than the oppressed? Who is better than both the living and the dead? Why?

By turning his attention to the cries of the oppressed, the Teacher shifts from the theoretical to the personal. This shift highlights a bleak reality: every act of injustice affects real people and is perpetuated by real people. When wickedness sits in the place of judgment, real people suffer.

But the situation is even worse. Not only has justice failed these oppressed people, but their community has also turned its back on them because those who harmed them were powerful. Consequently, there is no hope for them to receive justice or expect people to come to their aid.

So helpless is the case of the oppressed that the Teacher ends his meditation in a very dark place. *If this is the way life works, he reasons, then what's the point of life? If no one will respond to your cries for help, what's the point of even having a voice? You're better off dead.* What the Teacher had previously deemed senseless, he now deems as evil. So evil, in fact, that it would be better to never even exist under the sun in the first place.

Think About It

Why do you think the Teacher has such a visceral reaction to oppression? Why do the cries of the oppressed send him into this existential tailspin?

Part of the answer might lie in how the powerful have weaponized *hevel*. While we struggle to navigate the limits of life under the sun, oppressors see those limits and manipulate them for their own benefit. Knowing justice has limits, they also know their actions will go unchecked. Knowing that having power means they can get away with evil, they indulge in it. Thus, they further the brokenness of the world, making it more *hevel* for others.

Yet, there is an irony here: the Teacher hears the cries of the oppressed and sees there is no one to comfort them while he is serving as the self-professed ruler in Israel. He is moved by their plight but does nothing to correct it. He does not combat it and simply offers detached commentary.

I've noticed a similar kind of numbing affect in my own life the last few years. Perhaps the shock of the brokenness of the world is wearing off. Or maybe it's being overwhelmed by my responsibilities. But I wonder if maybe it's the sheer amount of injustice I'm exposed to in a given day—wars in far off places, the struggles of friends from around the country, and losses closer to home. I have a hard time differentiating between which suffering requires my attention and which doesn't. Thus overwhelmed, I just shut down.

Scientists suggest this numbness is likely rooted in the fact that our brains have a hard time conceptualizing large numbers.[19] We can process individual losses and empathize at an emotional level with the grief an individual family might be experiencing. But when the numbers rise, we lose our ability to empathize individually. We also lose some motivation needed to resist evil. This means feelings alone shouldn't determine whether we act against injustice. Nor should we feel responsible to respond to every injustice that floods our newsfeed. But perhaps it does mean asking God *how* to respond, trusting Someone beyond our own sensibilities to guide us.

Think About It

Have you ever felt that a problem was so big it was impossible to solve? How did this affect your desire to face it, combat it, or resist it? How might withdrawal or detachment to injustice be a kind of shortcut in an overwhelming world? What might be a better response?

TEARS OF THE OPPRESSED

Even though both we and the Teacher struggle to respond to injustice, God does not. In fact, Israel's own history rests on God hearing the cries of the oppressed. As Exodus 3:9-10 (ESV) says,

> And now, behold, the cry of the people of Israel has come to me [God], and I have also seen the oppression with which the Egyptians oppress them. Come, I will send you [Moses] to Pharaoh that you may bring my people, the children of Israel, out of Egypt.

So certain is God's attentiveness to those who suffer that the Black Church has found a unique solidarity in Israel's story of deliverance. To provide context, the Black Church is rooted in the worship gatherings of enslaved Africans. This religious institution, historically made up of seven major Black Protestant denominations in the United States, was formed in the late 1700s for Black Americans who were denied freedom and equality in the churches of white Americans. Author Elizabeth Woodson writes "Amidst the terrors of slavery, Jim Crow laws, racism, and discrimination, the Black Church has been a safe space of refuge, providing for the spiritual, social, educational, economic, and political needs of Black Christians."[20]

While waiting generations for their own deliverance from unjust laws and unspeakable atrocities, the Black Church has found hope in the promise that God hears their cries even if no one else does. The result is a rich heritage of sermons, hymns, poetry, and writing that witnesses to both earthly suffering and the dignity that comes from trusting God's faithfulness. In fact, many songs now sung in churches around the world—songs like "He's Got the Whole World in His Hands" and "Standing in the Need of Prayer"—teach us how to live while waiting for the day when God's justice will "flow like water, and righteousness, like an unfailing stream" (Amos 5:24).

RIGHTEOUSNESS BEFORE GOD (PART 1)

After considering how injustice affects individuals, the Teacher turns to the question of personal righteousness. How should we as unjust human beings relate to a just and righteous God?

READ ECCLESIASTES 5:1-7.

What posture does the Teacher recommend when approaching God?

What does the Teacher say God prefers over sacrifice?

What are the Teacher's instructions about making vows and commitments to God?

Initially this passage doesn't appear to be addressing injustice. But remember the Scripture links justice and righteousness very closely. In this text, our personal righteousness is revealed by how we approach God and whether we keep our word to Him. Do we understand the seriousness of making promises? Do we fulfill what we say we will do?

Knowing the human tendency toward injustice, the Teacher cautions us to approach God with humility and seriousness. In fact, according to the Teacher, it's better to be less religiously fervent—not make vows—than to make vows we're not going to keep. We need to remember that how we relate to God is directly connected to how we relate to others.

If our neighbors see us break a promise *to God*, why would they trust us to keep our word to them? Worse, if we claim to be God's people, what does our lack of righteousness say about God?

So the Teacher concludes in much the same way as he did in Ecclesiastes 3: The surest route to justice and keeping our word is to "fear God." We must humble ourselves before Him, obey His commands, and keep our word—to God and others.

Think About It

When was a time you made an impulsive promise or commitment to God? How did it work out? Did you regret it later? What did you learn from the experience?

Our family experienced the weight of an impulsive promise about a decade ago. Over several years we moved from place to place, always living in rentals that wouldn't allow pets. However, that didn't stop our children from begging for one. Eventually, out of desperation, we promised that "when we get our own house with a fence and a yard, we'll get a dog." About a year later, we bought our first house. As you might imagine, our kids did not forget our promise. However, we weren't quite ready to fulfill it. But then we remembered Psalm 15:4b that says God honors "those who fear the LORD, who keeps his word whatever the cost." So we found a sweet, young beagle named Cal at The Society for the Prevention of Cruelty to Animals and brought him home—a very unfortunate decision for everyone.

For the next eighteen months, we struggled as new dog owners. We couldn't keep Cal in the fence, nor settle on who was responsible for his care. We quickly discovered we were in over our heads. Fortunately, a family friend who'd just returned from overseas ministry was looking for a dog to join their small family to help them transition back home. It was a perfect fit. Looking back, I still feel the humbling sting of making a commitment that we weren't quite ready to fulfill. But I also see God's grace and kindness to everyone involved. Our family cared for Cal until he found his permanent home— blessing our friend and her family in exactly the way they needed it.

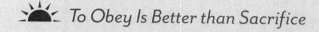 ## To Obey Is Better than Sacrifice

In Ecclesiastes 5:1, the Teacher warns that it is better to fulfill our word and approach God in humble obedience than to come brashly into God's presence thinking that our sacrifices or expressions of religious devotion can make up for our disobedience. This theme permeates the Old Testament.

For example, in 1 Samuel 15, God sent Saul to fight against the Amalekites. He promised Saul victory but warned him to not keep any spoils of the battle. Instead of obeying, however, Saul rashly decided to keep the best of the herds, stating that his plan was to sacrifice them to the Lord. The prophet Samuel confronted him with these pointed words:

Does the LORD *take pleasure in burnt offerings and sacrifices as much as in obeying the* LORD*?*
Look: to obey is better than sacrifice,
to pay attention is better than the fat of rams.

1 SAMUEL 15:22

Several other OT passages pick up this theme (see Ps. 40:6; 51:16). But the prophet Amos tied it directly to injustice. God confronted the people for their failure to obey His commands to treat others justly, saying:

Even though you bring me burnt offerings and grain offerings,
I will not accept them.

Though you bring choice fellowship offerings,
I will have no regard for them.

Away with the noise of your songs!
I will not listen to the music of your harps.

But let justice roll on like a river,
righteousness like a never-failing stream!

AMOS 5:22-24, NIV

IMPULSIVE IDEALISM VS. PRINCIPLED PRAGMATISM

READ ECCLESIASTES 5:8-9.

The Teacher says that when we see oppression or injustice we shouldn't be astonished.

> Why do you think the Teacher feels compelled to combat our naiveté? What is the risk of remaining naive to oppression?

> According to the Teacher, what is one reason the oppression of the poor and injustice continues? Think this is still true today? Explain.

This section is a good example of the Teacher's pragmatism—and one reason Ecclesiastes can feel so uncomfortable to our modern ears. As in this text, the Teacher often appears to be making concessions to a crooked world. By stating and acknowledging the way the world works, it sometimes sounds like he is accepting and condoning it. And rather than attempting to change it for the better, he seems concerned with finding whatever happiness he can. But don't we all have a responsibility to make the world a better place? If we see injustice, shouldn't we say something?

Part of what the Teacher is wrestling with is the limits of human ability to make a difference in this world. While his wisdom is deeply pragmatic, it is not necessarily unprincipled. He has a keen sense of what can and can't be accomplished, then makes decisions in light of it—all within the expectation that judgment is in God's hands. All within the expectation that he himself will be judged by God someday.

In this sense, the Teacher adopts a kind of "principled pragmatism"—a realistic view of the world with humble obedience forming its boundaries. He doesn't take advantage of brokenness, but he also doesn't expect to conquer injustice himself—or in himself. Instead, the Teacher operates within the limits of life under the sun, waiting for the day when God "will bring every act to judgment, including every hidden thing, whether good or evil" (Eccl. 12:14).

GOSPEL CONNECTION

In Matthew 6:9-10 (NIV), Jesus taught His disciples to pray in this way:

> *Our Father in heaven,*
> *hallowed be your name,*
> *your kingdom come,*
> *your will be done,*
> *on earth as it is in heaven.*

One of the striking things about Jesus's ministry is the degree to which He simultaneously confronted injustice while also embracing the limits of life under the sun. Despite His power to do miracles, He did not heal everyone. Despite His power to liberate, He did not free Israel from political oppression. And despite His ability to redeem, He did not immediately save the world.

In this way, Jesus was kind of a disappointment to people who expected the Messiah to fix everything quickly and neatly. Instead, Jesus entrusted the world to the Father, praying the Father's will would be done on earth.

Then Jesus rolled up His sleeves and obeyed the Father, doing the work that He had been given to do. Or as Philippians 2 puts it,

> *And when he had come as a man,*
> *he humbled himself by becoming obedient*
> *to the point of death—*
> *even to death on a cross.*

PHILIPPIANS 2:7b-8

In the infinite wisdom of God, our own justification came from Jesus's obedience to the Father's will.

By His obedience, Jesus makes us the kind of people who can participate in the ongoing work of justice. A work we carry out the same way He did— through faithful obedience and trust in the Father's plan.

RIGHTEOUSNESS BEFORE GOD (PART II)

The Teacher continues his reflections on justice and righteousness by facing the reality that even when we commit to being just, it still escapes us.

READ ECCLESIASTES 7:15-18.

What painful ironic reality does the Teacher highlight in verse 15?

What conclusion does the Teacher reach after realizing that the righteous aren't necessarily saved from suffering and death while the wicked sometimes enjoy long, prosperous lives (vv. 16-17)?

How would you explain verses 16-17? Do you agree with this advice? Why or why not?

The key to understanding this complicated (and uncomfortable) passage lies in remembering the Teacher's goal and assumptions. He is trying to make sense of life "under the sun." He wants to know why a person would pursue righteousness if there's no guarantee that righteousness will be rewarded and evil will be punished in this life.

It's an entirely fair question. The Teacher eventually concludes that righteousness won't necessarily make your life easier, longer, or more enjoyable. In fact, sometimes the opposite happens—the righteous struggle while the wicked seem to prosper. Since the benefits of righteousness are unpredictable in this life, the Teacher decides that the way forward is to not do anything "excessively." But the Teacher's advice isn't about leading a balanced life so much as highlighting a deeper, more painful reality about life under the sun: *You can't count on your righteousness to keep you safe.*

The question is not whether we *should* be righteous but whether we can trust our righteousness to protect us. The answer—at least according to the Teacher—is that we can't. So we must recognize its limits and live within them. We must recognize that this life alone will not reward goodness or punish evil.

☀ *The Paradox of Scripture*

The Teacher's words in this passage seem to go against other passages of Scripture. For example, Proverbs 11:1-19 teaches that pursuing righteousness leads to success and safety—"The righteous one is rescued from trouble; in his place, the wicked one goes in" (v. 8). These kinds of tensions are why some people say the Bible contradicts itself. But instead of contradictions, it might be better to understand these differences as contributions—each text contributing something slightly different to the conversation of faith. Rather than pit Proverbs and Ecclesiastes against each other in debate, we better understand them as in dialogue. Each book, in its own way, is offering something true about life on earth, and we must consider both to gain a complete picture. In this sense, we should read them as, "Yes, and . . ." Yes, it's true that pursuing righteousness can keep you from certain difficulties, and it's also true that righteousness cannot keep you from all difficulty. In this way, the Bible speaks holistically and honestly about the paradox of life itself.

Think About It

In what ways do you find yourself counting on good choices or proper behavior to keep you safe from suffering and death? Does the fact that your personal righteousness cannot completely protect you change how you understand the Teacher's advice to not be "excessively righteous" or "overly wise"? Explain.

READ ECCLESIASTES 7:19-20.

After he recognizes that righteous living doesn't save us from suffering and death, the Teacher takes it one step further. He questions whether any of us can actually *be* righteous in the first place. Maybe the problem isn't simply that this life doesn't reward righteousness; maybe the problem is that we can't be righteous even if it did.

With verse 20, the Teacher hits rock bottom in his pursuit of justice under the sun. No matter how careful we are, no matter how much we resist injustice, no matter how much we desire to be righteous ourselves, "there is certainly no one righteous on the earth who does good and never sins."

Read the following passages, and write how each text confirms what the Teacher said.

PSALM 53:1	
ECCLESIASTES 7:20	
ROMANS 3:10	
ROMANS 3:23	
1 JOHN 1:8	

UNEXPECTEDLY GOOD NEWS

Today's passage is another example of how Ecclesiastes corrects our questions and prepares us to receive the answers we need—even if the answers aren't fully satisfying. The Teacher enters his examination of justice observing that the world is fundamentally "not right"—it is *hevel*. Even our best attempts to bring about justice are corrupted. By forcing us to face the pervasiveness of injustice and our own unrighteousness, we're pushed to a place of honesty about our utter helplessness. Once we're there, we're finally in a place to embrace God's grace. After all, forgiveness only makes sense to people who know they need it.

Think About It

In what ways is the truth that no one is righteous both freeing and convicting?

READ ECCLESIASTES 7:21-22.

What does the Teacher suggest you do when you hear someone talking about you—especially if that person holds less authority than you do?

Why does the Teacher suggest that you overlook or ignore this kind of slight?

The Teacher's advice to overlook minor offenses is rooted in the larger logic of this section. When we realize that "there is certainly no one righteous on the earth" (v. 20), we have to admit that we too are not righteous. Admitting this frees us to receive God's grace, but it also empowers us to extend grace to others. One way we do that is by not looking for things to be offended by—and by not being offended when we find them.

As an example, the Teacher says: "Don't pay attention to everything people say." Another way to phrase this might be, "Don't take what people say to heart." Why? Because someone, somewhere, sometime has probably said something unkind or untrue about you. And before you get all upset about it, remember that you only know it's a possibility because you've done the exact same thing yourself.

In this way, recognizing the limits of our own righteousness humbles us and prepares us to respond to both major and minor offenses properly. If, on the other hand, we maintain a false sense of our righteousness—if we believe that our works are somehow the source of our stability and safety—then we're bound to get our pride hurt when we hear someone speaking negatively about us. When that happens, we're likely to lash out in anger and self-justification.

But when we humbly remember our own sin, we'll be reminded we've been forgiven. And we'll find ourselves able to forgive others.

ETERNAL JUSTICE

How should we respond to the reality of injustice in the world and in our own hearts? What hope do we have that this will all be made right?

READ ECCLESIASTES 8:9-11.

What does the Teacher observe about how the wicked are received in holy places?

According to the Teacher, what is one reason people are tempted to do evil (v. 11)?

In this passage, the Teacher turned his attention to wickedness in religious contexts, recognizing that as much as evil is prevalent in both civil and personal life, it also invades the "holy place." Not only were the wicked praised in the city where they perpetrated their evil deeds, they were also allowed to participate in religious life without correction or exhibiting repentance. Instead of being condemned, they are esteemed. This in turn leads to more wickedness when people realize the wicked won't be held accountable for their actions.

Think About It

Do you expect religious contexts to be free from injustice or unrighteousness? How do your assumptions shape your response when you hear about sin in religious contexts? How might a previous experience affect your disposition—either positively or negatively?

☀ Creating Cultures of Righteousness & Justice

"Because the sentence against an evil act is not carried out quickly, the heart of people is filled with the desire to commit evil" (Eccl. 8:11).

Two natural responses to injustice are to look the other way or delay addressing it. But the Teacher warned that these kind of responses can create a culture of moral ambiguity. When injustice goes unchecked, people begin to lose a sense of right and wrong. Or, as some have summarized this dilemma: "What you condone, sets the tone" and "What you tolerate, you encourage."

Ultimately, this moral confusion leads to a reversal of the very definitions of righteousness and wickedness. When wickedness is rewarded, people are conditioned to believe it is goodness. And when goodness is punished, they view it as wickedness. That's why it's important we stand against injustices in our own communities. The consequences of doing so goes beyond a specific incident. It affects culture.

Despite the Teacher's brutal assessment, however, he does not completely give up on being righteous. Instead, he seems to recalibrate how and when he expects to see righteousness rewarded.

READ ECCLESIASTES 8:12-15.

In verses 12-13, how does the Teacher seem to reverse his previous assessment about the end of the wicked and the "God-fearing"? What was the defining feature between the two groups?

Compare verses 12-13 and verse 14. Despite apparent contradictions, what might explain how the Teacher could believe that things will "go well" for the God-fearing while also saying that righteous people sometimes are punished on earth?

Given all this, what was the Teacher's final conclusion in verse 15?

When we fear God and look to Him to establish justice, we can live in the hope that all will one day work out as it should—if not in this life then in the next.

While it might look like the Teacher is speaking out of both sides of his mouth (again), a close reading of this passage helps us understand his underlying logic. Verses 12-13 introduce God into the conversation while verse 14 speaks of what happens "on the earth." In other words, when we fear God and look to Him to establish justice, we can live in the hope that all will one day work out as it should—if not in this life then in the next. But when justice is left to people alone, when we pin our hope on people, we shouldn't be surprised when the righteous are punished and the wicked are set free.

The Fugitive Slave Act passed by Congress in 1850 is one example of how human justice can get completely turned upside down. The law said that even if a slave managed to escape her captors and make it to a free state, it was required she be returned to her owners! What this law defined as a moral responsibility—returning a person to captivity—was actually a deeply unjust and immoral act. But because it was legal, it had the guise of righteousness and respectability. As a result, officers of the state could participate in an evil act in clear conscience because, after all, they were only "following the law." But lest we look back on history and feel superior, upside down "justice" is common in human society even today. Instead of asking *whether* we currently name evil as good, it would be better to ask "what" and "how" does our society name evil as good.

The reality that the righteous are punished and the wicked set free finds its ultimate climax in the crucifixion of Jesus: The religious establishment rejected a righteous man while rewarding wicked men for falsely accusing him. Powerful people exchanged bribes and favors. Despite being innocent, Jesus was condemned and Barabbas, a guilty man, went free. Meanwhile, the justice system washed its hands of Him, incapable or unwilling to do the very thing they were tasked with doing. He was taken, oppressed, and His cries unheard. No one stopped what was happening. So, between two thieves, the life of the innocent was cut short, hung where the guilty should be.

While Christians understand the death of Jesus to be on our behalf, it's important that we don't rush past the injustice of the moment too quickly. The death of Jesus was a profoundly unjust act perpetuated by an unjust world. It is the ultimate expression of *hevel*.

So we must stop and consider: *If even the son of God was punished for righteousness, what does this mean for our lives under the sun? If even the Son of God could not escape injustice, can we? How can we live in a world that does not recognize goodness when it was standing right in front of it?*

UNEXPECTEDLY GOOD NEWS

In our text yesterday, the Teacher wrestled with the fact that death does not differentiate between the righteous and unrighteous. Both die. So, like the righteous, the unjust can't escape it. Death will surely put an end to their evil and will also deliver them to God and judgment.

Read the following verses, and summarize the overall message from the passages.

Ecclesiastes 9:1

Ecclesiastes 11: 9

Ecclesiastes 12:7,13-14

Together, these texts echo Hebrews 9:27-28.

> *And just as it is appointed for people to die once — and after this, judgment — so also Christ, having been offered once to bear the sins of many, will appear a second time, not to bear sin, but to bring salvation to those who are waiting for him.*

In other words, our ability to live in an unjust world rests on our hope that this world is not all there is. Instead, we need a hope beyond death. We need the hope of a just Judge.

First Peter 2 tells us that this hope is exactly how Jesus survived the *hevel* of life under the sun.

> *For you were called to this, because Christ also suffered for you, leaving you an example, that you should follow in his steps. He did not commit sin, and no deceit was found in his mouth; when he was insulted, he did not insult in return; when he suffered, he did not threaten but entrusted himself to the one who judges justly.*

1 PETER 2:21-23

Just as Jesus entrusted Himself to the Father throughout His life, He entrusted Himself to the Father in His death. So that when the time came, He could confidently surrender His spirit to the Father, knowing that He would judge justly. And that's exactly what the Father did. When God raised Jesus from the dead three days later, all the world knew that He was righteous. And the power of *hevel* was broken for good.

REFLECTION

Session 7

*Below you'll find some questions to help you think through
and apply what you've learned in this week of study.
Be prepared to discuss these if you're doing the study in a group.*

1   **Which day of study this week was your favorite and why?**

2   **How would you summarize the Teacher's view of justice under the sun?**

3   **How does this compare to what Jesus and the New Testament writers taught about justice under the sun?**

4   **What are the main takeaways for you from this week and how do they apply to your life?**

*If you're leading a group, check out the leader guide
found at lifeway.com/lifeunderthesun.*

Session 8

TIME UNDER
THE SUN

In the final week, we will look at how the Teacher faced the temporary nature of our lives "under the sun." We are beings bound by time facing a certain end. As a result, some people simply surrender to the wheels of time and embrace a kind of fatalism. Others will do everything in their power to resist death and aging. But neither of these answers can satisfy, and neither is the way of Christ. Through His resurrection, Jesus frees us from the threat of time, even as we continue to live out our lives in different seasons. Ultimately our confidence rests in the God who one day will bring everything to resolution within Himself.

TIMES AND SEASONS

As we finish our study of Ecclesiastes, we'll consider the question of time. What exactly should we do with the days we've been given? How should we move through them?

READ ECCLESIASTES 1:5-7.

How does verse 5 describe the sun's journey of rising and setting? What emotions does it convey?

How might these natural phenomenon of sun, wind, and water relate to our understanding of time and activity?

We looked at this passage in Week 1, but we're returning to it today to remember how time functions in Ecclesiastes. Throughout the book, there is a tension between measuring time through its cycles (e.g., the sun's rising and setting) and measuring whether we're actually getting anywhere. Time may be passing, but is it moving us forward? Is it moving us closer to our hopes and dreams?

In this passage, the Narrator uses natural phenomenon to frame up that tension. Rather than moving along a linear path, our lives are like the sun or wind, orbiting and cycling their way through time. But this turning doesn't always feel productive; it can often feel like we're spinning in circles.

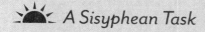 ## A Sisyphean Task

The ancient Greek myth of Sisyphus echoes the underlying frustration of Ecclesiastes 1:5-7. After escaping death, Hades condemned Sisyphus to repeatedly roll a stone to the top of a hill only to have it roll back down again. For eternity. And so Sisyphus spent his days repeating the same action over and over again and seeing no progress for it.

This is similar to the way Ecclesiastes 1 depicts the work of nature. The sun rushes back and forth across the sky only to have to get up the next day and do it all again. The wind makes a complete circuit from north to south, only to find itself in the same place as where it started. And even though the streams flow to the sea, the sea is never filled. So the streams must keep flowing.

Both the Sisyphean myth and this section of text evoke feelings of helplessness, despair, and futility. In fact, we still use this language today. When something is both hard and pointless, we call it a Sisyphean task.

Think About It

How do the repetitive movements of celestial bodies—the sun, moon, and stars—structure our own sense of time and timekeeping? How do the seasons affect our sense of forward movement and expectation?

READ ECCLESIASTES 3:1-8.

What observation does verse 1 make about time?

What pattern do you observe about the pairs in verses 2-8?

Do you think these pairs are prescriptive, telling the reader what he or she should do, or descriptive, just describing what happens? Explain your answer.

Ecclesiastes 3 is one of the most famous sections of the book, if not the whole Bible. These verses have inspired poets and artists from Johannes Brahms to Pete Seeger, the latter using them as the basis of the popular song "Turn! Turn! Turn!" The lilting verses of this poem offer us several examples of Hebrew poetry structure, including parallelism, merism, and envelope or chiasmic structure.

First, we see parallelism in the text's consistent, repeated form:

"a time to __A__ and a time to __B__."

After the introduction in verse 1, every line of the poem uses this underlying shape of contrasting pairs.

A time **to give birth** and a time **to die**

A time **to plant** and a time **to uproot**

A time **to kill** and a time **to heal**

A time **to tear down** and a time **to build**, etc.

These pairs also function as merisms in which opposites represent both themselves and everything in between. For example, verse 4 says there is "a time to give birth and a time to die" marking the beginning and end points of human life. But in between those points, human existence is marked by a whole spectrum of growth and change. The poem is using the extremes to represent the whole, speaking to all the different events that happen in life.

The poem also uses an envelope structure or chiasmus to join different lines together. Consider verse 8:

A time to **love** and a time to **hate**;

A time for **war** and a time for **peace**

You'll see that the second line repeats the first by making it more specific: love becomes peace while hatred leads to war. But the order is also switched so that the lines read:

Line 1: love (A) hate (B)

Line 2: war (B*) peace(A*)

Visually, this ABBA structure creates an "X" which is also the shape of the Greek letter *chi*—thus a chiasmus.

And so, it seems that time and nature are not the only things that shift back and forth in rhythmic ways. Poetic form does as well.

CONTINUE READING ECCLESIASTES 3:9-15.

According to verse 11, who makes everything for its specific time? How does this affect our understanding of the cycles and patterns of life?

What do you think it means that God has put eternity in each person's heart?

What is the Teacher's advice for navigating the different patterns of time?

In contrast to earthly cycles, how does verse 14 describe God's work?

As the Teacher reflects on the meaning of this poem, he notes that God is the one who made time to work in seasonal, cyclical ways. In fact, Genesis 1 suggests this reality is built into the very fabric of creation:

> *Then God said, "Let there be lights in the expanse of the sky to separate the day from the night. They will serve as signs for seasons and for days and years. They will be lights in the expanse of the sky to provide light on the earth." And it was so.*

GENESIS 1:14-15

Just as God ordained time to play out in patterns and rhythms in nature, our lives have patterns and seasons as well. Part of becoming wise means learning to recognize the season we're currently in and attuning ourselves to what God is doing in that season. Because, as the Teacher notes, these cycles have a trajectory beyond themselves—they are carrying us on to eternity (v. 11).

> *In the day of prosperity be joyful, but in the day of adversity, consider: God has made the one as well as the other so no one can discover anything that will come after him.*

ECCLESIASTES 7:14

SPINNING TOWARD GOD

Despite the repetitive nature of life under the sun, we know we are heading toward something. We realize there is more to life than simply moving in circles. One way to conceptualize this truth is to think of how a record player works. If you watch a record on a turntable, it appears to simply be turning in circles. But only the record and record player are fixed in a specific place in time; the needle is not. It moves closer and closer to the center by means of microscopic grooves that spiral inward from the outside edge of the record, unlocking music with every turn.

So too, our lives under the sun can feel like they're spinning in circles. We find ourselves in the same place, facing the same challenges, asking the same questions, over and over again. But with each cycle, with each turn, we're moving closer and closer to the center. Each season, each turn of the sun, God is drawing us to Himself.

If you could uncoil the groove of a typical LP record, it would measure 1,500 feet per side!

PAST, PRESENT, FUTURE

Even as time cycles, it moves forward. There is a relationship between past, present, and future—one we inhabit both as individuals and as communities.

READ ECCLESIASTES 1:9-11.

How does the word *new* evoke a sense of time?

What words in verses 9-11 signal the following:

The past

The present

The future

During the first week of our study, we considered this text through the lens of what we remember and what we forget. But remembering and forgetting are features of time and our place in it. By definition, remembering means recalling something that *has* happened, something we learned or experienced *before* this moment. Correspondingly, verse 11 speaks of what will happen—what *will* follow this moment in the future.

In this way, Ecclesiastes 1:9-11 speaks to a reality we often take for granted: While time has a circular quality, it also is linear. Any given moment has a past, present, and future. This may seem like an obvious statement, but it's an important one—especially for people who exist in a culture with a strong preference for the present.

One of the oddities of living in our contemporary moment is the degree to which everything is, well, contemporary. In the modern west, we spend a great deal of time keeping up with current events and trends. We chase pop culture and try to keep up to date. But the present is a moving target. For example, just when we've figured out how to adopt a trending hairstyle, it goes out of fashion. If we continue wearing it, we date ourselves.

Our fixation with the present can also blind us to the past and future. On one hand, we can forget we have a past. We don't know our heritage or our roots. In fact, when we want to dismiss something as not relevant, we claim that it's "history"—as if the past didn't have a direct bearing on our lives today.

A generation goes and a generation comes, but the earth remains forever.

Ecclesiastes 1:4

At the same time, living exclusively in the present—prioritizing our pressing wants, desires, and interests—can cause us to forget that the future will come. Whatever we sow today will come to harvest tomorrow. So even as we live in the moment, we must orient ourselves to both past and future. We must understand ourselves as creatures bound by time.

Think About It

Think of a cultural trend or fashion you adopted in high school. In the moment, why was it important for you to embrace this latest thing? How important is it to you now? Explain.

ORIENTING TIME

Part of being a creature bound by time means learning to make decisions in light of our past, present, and future. But to do so means knowing how to think about each of these seasons. Fortunately, the Teacher gives some practical advice for properly relating to time.

Look up the following verses to see how Ecclesiastes conceptualizes the past, present, and future. Summarize the wisdom and implications in your own words. (Look up the verses in different translations to help with this activity.)

Ecclesiastes 1:9; 6:10

Ecclesiastes 7:10

Ecclesiastes 9:1b

Ecclesiastes 10:14

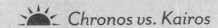 *Chronos vs. Kairos*

In English, we use the word *time* to describe both chronological timekeeping and specific moments. *Time* has both a quantitative meaning (e.g, recording days, hours, years, etc.) and a qualitative meaning (e.g, "the right time" or "a bad time" for something to occur). This can sometimes cause us to miss the underlying meaning of different texts.

Both ancient Hebrew and biblical Greek, on the other hand, have multiple words for *time* to help differentiate between chronological time and opportune time. In the New Testament, these ideas are represented by the words *chronos* and *kairos* respectively. In Ecclesiastes, you'll find both ideas as well. When the Teacher spoke about the brevity of life, he is operating in chronological time. But when he speaks of different seasons of time, he is operating in opportune time—a moment when all the circumstances are aligned for a particular action.

There is often a tension between *chronos* and *kairos*—one that comes forward in this week's study. Just because the calendar says it's time for something to happen doesn't mean the circumstances are right for it to happen. For instance, just because the calendar says it's the first day of spring doesn't mean the elements are right to put your seeds in the ground. Part of living wisely under the sun means learning to distinguish between the two.

THE TIMELESS ONE

While we struggle to orient ourselves to time under the sun, there is One who exists beyond both the sun and time. To wisely engage past, present, and future, we must admit that our sense of time is not the ultimate reality, even if it is the reality we inhabit. Instead, we must recognize that God is working out His own purposes along His own time line.

READ 2 PETER 3:2-9.

Why do scoffers think that God has not fulfilled His promise? What argument do they make based on time (vv. 3-4)?

According to verse 8, what important fact do scoffers overlook?

How does verse 9 redefine "delay"?

What is the goal of God's patience throughout time?

Remembering. Forgetting. Anticipating. Expecting. Waiting. Hoping.

All of these movements speak to the reality of our existence as creatures bound by time. But we are not at the mercy of time—at least not when we entrust ourselves to the One who is eternal.

This recently became tangible for me—returning to school after twenty plus years out of the classroom. In God's plan, I married and started a family young, forgoing opportunities for post-graduate work. The shape of the contemporary marketplace and the demands of family life also meant I delayed pursuing my vocation as a writer until after my children entered school. For a long time, I worried about the choices I'd made. I never regretted prioritizing my family in those early years, but I also knew other people had made different choices. Plus, I was certain I wasn't done cultivating my work outside our home—in some sense, I hadn't even really started. Eventually, I began writing and bit by bit, found myself an author. And today, I'm actively pursuing a graduate degree at a top-tier school—an opportunity my twenty-something self could never have imagined possible.

Some might see my story as happening in reverse, that I'm finally getting to do what I should have been able to do twenty years ago. But I don't think of returning to school as reclaiming my youth. This would suggest that I missed something—that all those years were somehow "less than" because I didn't follow a socially-prescribed and expected path. Instead, I'm learning to trust that my current opportunities are coming at just the right time, that I'm exactly the student I need to be at this moment to learn exactly the things I need to learn. And that it couldn't have come a moment sooner. This doesn't mean everyone should wait to pursue schooling or that I wouldn't advise my own children differently. It simply means I'm learning to make peace with the fact that God works on His own timetable, which is different for each of us. In this, we can be confident that God—and not some arbitrary work of time—has brought us exactly where we need to be when we need to be there.

Think About It

How has your awareness of the past, present, and future changed over the years? How does your awareness of the past and the future affect your present decisions? How does God and His purposes factor into your decision making?

TIME UNPREDICTABLE

As we begin to understand the shape and movement of time, we try to orient ourselves within it. But how can you orient yourself to something that isn't completely predictable?

READ ECCLESIASTES 8:6-9.

How does verse 7 challenge and expand verse 6?

The theme of authority comes up repeatedly in these verses, especially regarding what we can command and what we can't. List at least two things that the text says we can't command.

What is a possible connection between time and the limits of our authority?

The larger context of this passage is about how to respond to those in authority over us. However, embedded within this conversation, the Teacher talks about the nature of time. He says, "For every activity there is a right time and procedure" (v. 6a). This counsel repeats the wisdom of chapter 3 that says "there is an occasion for everything, and a time for every activity under heaven" (3:1).

But then, verse 7 takes a surprising turn. Despite there being a right time and procedure for every activity, we don't know what time that is. There's no guarantee that our actions in this moment—although perfectly-timed and executed—will result in future success. We can no more control the future than we can control the wind or the day of our birth. This challenges one of the myths of modern life: we believe we can master time.

After all, we can observe patterns and trends. We can chart cycles. We can synthesize data and make educated guesses about what will happen in three, five, and ten years. Then, based on that information, we make investments believing they will pay out a certain amount just when we need it. We map out our careers, pinpointing the precise day we can retire with the most benefits. We optimize our schedules, hoping to wring out every possible ounce of productivity and fun from our lives.

While none of these practices are wrong, they can offer a false sense of security. The success of these strategies depend on everything staying the same and going according to plan. No unexpected variations, no illnesses, no problems. No global pandemics or wars.

But when these events break into our world, we find ourselves facing our limits.

Think About It

What is your approach to time management? What do you expect your scheduling and productivity apps to deliver? To what degree might FOMO ("fear of missing out") drive your approach to time and how much you expect to get done?

TIME WELL SPENT

In many ways, our drive for productivity is rooted in trying to get as much from life as possible. After all, as Ecclesiastes reminds us often, death is coming. So if we're going to do something, we'd better get to it. What are we to make of this tension? How can we honor our lack of control over time while also honoring the shortness of our days under the sun?

READ ECCLESIASTES 9:4-10.

Summarize how the Teacher illustrated and explained the advantage the living have over the dead (vv. 4-6)?

What was the Teacher's counsel to the living about enjoying their lives under the sun?

As he did previously, the Teacher circles back to consider the other side of the question. Even though the future is unpredictable, we shouldn't give up planning, working, or dreaming. In fact, the shortness of our lives means we *should* work, plan, and dream all the more because one day, we won't be able to. In other words, the limits of time should motivate us to use it well. And so, the Teacher counseled us in two ways:

1. "Enjoy... all the days of your fleeting life" (v. 9a)

and

2. "Whatever your hands find to do, do with all your strength" (v. 10a)

Once we understand the limits of our power, we can use whatever power we do have effectively. Once we understand we can't manage time, we can live within it well, using it as a partner to accomplish the work God has given us to do.

Think About It

What plans or goals have you put off to "someday"? Does considering the shortness of life change your perspective on moving forward with them? Explain.

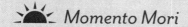 **Momento Mori**

It is better to go to a house of mourning than to go to a house of feasting, since that is the end of mankind and the living should take it to heart.

ECCLESIASTES 7:2

While modern society tends to shun reminders of death, with these words the Teacher actively invites us to remember ours.

This may sound morbid to contemporary society, but prior to modern medicine, death was a constant companion to life. Funeral rites and burial rituals were common community affairs, so humans lived with a nearly constant awareness of death.

Sayings like Ecclesiastes 7:2 fall under the call to *momento mori* or to "remember death." This Latin phrase is used to describe art works and motifs that represent death. They include things like skulls and skeletons on gravestones and vanitas paintings of the Northern Renaissance. In these still-life scenes, artists represented flowers in various stages of decay to remind viewers of their own short lives.

The Teacher reminded us that it is good to look death in the face. This act of remembering our days under the sun will soon end pushes us to decide how we want to use them.

CREATURES OF TIME

There is clearly a paradox between accepting that we cannot manage time and using our time well. Our lives play out in the middle of this tension. But we do not need to fear it or let it paralyze us. Instead, we must learn to live in the reality of both truths: Time is not ours to master, and time is ours to use.

I'm sympathetic to the underlying questions and I've asked them myself countless times: *Have I used my time well? Should I have done something different with my life?* But instead of viewing these questions as a crisis, I'm learning to trust that God might intend them as opportunities for metamorphosis. Instead of worrying about how I used my time in the past, I find myself wondering how I want to use the time that I have left. As I get older, how I choose to use my time becomes increasingly important.

But instead of wanting to do more with my days, I find myself wanting to do less—and to do it well. This has birthed an unexpected clarity and focus in my life. I find that I'm able to say no with greater ease, especially when a project or opportunity doesn't move me along the path that I believe God is leading me down. But instead of managing time, I find that I'm managing myself. I'm managing my vocation, my attention, and my commitments. And suddenly, I find myself less worried about getting it all done, and more focused on getting my work done.

Throughout His earthly ministry, Jesus embodied the tension of how to best use His days on the earth. While Galatians 4:4 speaks of His birth as happening when "time came to completion" (CSB), He became subject to the limits of time under the sun. He had to wait for redemption's plan to unfold. He knew that there was an hour or moment in which His calling would come to fruition, but He regularly had to tell others that it was "not yet" (See also John 2:4; 7:6,8).

But as He waited, He worked and enjoyed the life given to Him. For thirty hidden years, He was an obedient son, with His life in Nazareth likely rotating around the simple, mundane routines of family, work, and community. Then, after He began His ministry, He healed, preached, worshiped, and feasted. By entrusting Himself to the care of the Father, He was free to live with joy and purpose. He counsels us to do the same:

> *Therefore I tell you: Don't worry about your life, what you will eat or what you will drink; or about your body, what you will wear . . . But seek first the kingdom of God and his righteousness, and all these things will be provided for you. Therefore, don't worry about tomorrow, because tomorrow will worry about itself.*

MATTHEW 6:25,33-34a

FROM AGE TO AGE

As we've seen, time both cycles and moves forward. But these movements are not abstract; we experience them in personal ways as we move through seasons of our lives. What would it look like to inhabit each season—whether youth or old age—with wisdom?

READ ECCLESIASTES 11:7-10.

What do you think "light" and "eyes seeing the sun" symbolize in verse 7? (Hint: Think about the imagery in relationship to Ecclesiastes's central phrase "under the sun.")

What two paradoxical things should we do if we live long lives (v. 8)?

What advice does the Teacher give young people specifically (v. 9)?

According to verse 10, why should we focus on delight rather than sorrow? Does this advice make sense to you? Why or why not?

The Teacher begins this section by celebrating long life but warns that it will bring more sorrow. After all, a long life means more of what life has to offer—both good and bad. He then turns to those in their early years. He tells the young to take joy, be glad, and follow their heart's desires. But he is not suggesting a life of hedonism so much as highlighting something we sometimes say ourselves: "Youth is wasted on the young."

One of the ironies of youth is that you cannot gain a right perspective on it. It's easy to think you will always be young. But from a place of age and maturity, the Teacher warns young people that this season goes by very quickly. So enjoy it while you have it.

For some, this advice may sound suspiciously secular, ignoring the needs of the world or the call to committed discipleship. After all, in young adulthood we set the direction of our lives, with many folks making decisions about who they will marry, what careers they will pursue, and who they will become. These kinds of decisions demand a level of seriousness and maturity. But for the Teacher, maturity as a young person means understanding how quickly youth passes. Wisdom means understanding the realities of youth as God-given and embracing them in appropriate ways. Because, as this entire study has shown us, life will get hard soon enough.

Think About It

As a youth, did you understood how fast life would pass? Explain. What would you change about your teen years if you could? Based on your own experience, what advice would you give to a young adult you're close to?

READ ECCLESIASTES 12:1-8.

With what command does the Teacher open this section of poetry and what does it mean?

This passage is highly imaginative, picturing old age and death through various types of decay. List at least five images that suggest decay or death.

This particular section of Ecclesiastes is among its most evocative and poetic. For nearly eleven chapters, the Teacher has been warning us of the certainty of death. Here in the final verses of the book, he paints a picture of it, using the image of a dilapidated house and abandoned estate to suggest an aging, dying body.

Scholars suggest this section operates at several different levels of text. Some verses are literal while others are metaphorical and even eschatological. This shows how much power poetry has to hold information in a condensed form. And while multiple levels of meaning are possible, they all point to this central theme: decay and death mark life under the sun. Whether it's a house, a nation, or even our own bodies, we cannot escape the certainty of *hevel*.

WHAT TO EXPECT

If you read chapter 11 with a tinge of sadness and longing—perhaps even regret—then chapter 12 is for you. Part of what the Teacher is suggesting is that your experience of adulthood as "days of adversity"(v. 1) is actually pretty normal. If the irony of youth is that it is wasted on the young, the irony of aging is that wisdom only comes through experience. Aging brings its own kind of disorientation and loss. Just when we feel like we're finally getting life sorted out, our bodies start to break down. Just when we realize how to make good choices, the fruit of our previous choices come to fruition.

Part of the trouble lies in how aging confronts our larger cultural narratives. In modern life, we tend to see time as uninterrupted progress toward goodness. Given enough time, we believe we can find answers to our problems. But as we've discovered (from the Teacher and our own experience), life under the sun doesn't work that way. Instead, time narrows our choices, breaks down our bodies, and funnels us toward death.

But what if the decay of aging is not something to be resisted? What if this process prepares us for something greater than life under the sun? What if the years are given to remind us that "the mere mortal is headed to his eternal home" (v. 5)?

Facing death this way not only challenges the human instinct of self-preservation, it also goes against contemporary norms to fight to extend life as long as possible. We're expected to . . . "not go gentle into that good night."[21]

But what if we could learn to welcome age, and even dying, as something that moves us closer to God?

I learned what this might look like while watching a friend face death recently. Her final, lingering days were spent in a kind of expectant wonder. Looking back, I marvel at how she kept faith, how her loved ones and community kept faith with her. As well wishes and memories flooded in, so too, did words of anticipation and hope.

Instead of raging against death, my friend had learned to look toward it with a welcome eye, trusting that it would deliver her to a far, far better place than any of us had yet known. And so I wonder if we might be able to learn the same. I wonder if we might even learn to dream about who we'll be on the other side. Until with the poet Robert Browning we can invite each other to . . .

> Grow old along with me!
>
> The best is yet to be,
>
> The last of life, for which the first was made:
>
> Our times are in His hand
>
> Who saith "A whole I planned,
>
> Youth shows but half; trust God: see all, nor be afraid!"[22]

Think About It

What are your emotions and thoughts about facing death? What shapes your view?

UNEXPECTEDLY GOOD NEWS

While Ecclesiastes offers a frank assessment of the challenges of aging, other wisdom literature highlights the goodness that only time can offer us.

Look up the following passages and summarize their messages about aging.

Job 12:12

Psalm 72:17-18

In many ways, life under the sun wears us down. Yes, we grow and learn, but eventually, we begin the descent toward our final end. But God rules over even this process, using it for our good and His glory. Bit by bit, ache by ache, we are being transformed for goodness we cannot yet imagine—a goodness that exists with Him beyond the sun.

Or as Paul puts it in 2 Corinthians:

> *Even though our outer person is being destroyed, our inner person is being renewed day by day. For our momentary light affliction is producing for us an absolutely incomparable eternal weight of glory. So we do not focus on what is seen, but on what is unseen. For what is seen is temporary, but what is unseen is eternal.*
>
> *2 CORINTHIANS 4:16b-18*

The Velveteen Rabbit

In Margery Williams's classic children story, *The Velveteen Rabbit*, a toy rabbit gradually becomes real through the power of self-sacrifice and divine love. Early in the book, an old skin horse explains to the rabbit what it means to be made real:

"Real isn't how you are made,' said the Skin Horse. 'It's a thing that happens to you. When a child loves you for a long, long time, not just to play with, but REALLY loves you, then you become Real.'

'Does it hurt?' asked the Rabbit.

'Sometimes,' said the Skin Horse, for he was always truthful. 'When you are Real you don't mind being hurt.'

'Does it happen all at once, like being wound up,' he asked, 'or bit by bit?'

'It doesn't happen all at once,' said the Skin Horse. 'You become. It takes a long time. That's why it doesn't happen often to people who break easily, or have sharp edges, or who have to be carefully kept. Generally, by the time you are Real, most of your hair has been loved off, and your eyes drop out and you get loose in the joints and very shabby. But these things don't matter at all, because once you are Real you can't be ugly, except to people who don't understand."[23]

FROM AGE TO AGE

Today, we return to the conclusion of Ecclesiastes to hear the Narrator's final thoughts. When all is said and done, after all our exploring and consideration, how should we use our time "under the sun"?

READ ECCLESIASTES 12:13-14.

Put in your own words the advice the Narrator gives in verse 13.

According to verse 14, why should everyone fear God and keep His commands? What's significant about Him judging both good and evil?

How does the Narrator's conclusion relate to the rest of the book? Does it feel consistent or inconsistent? Why?

THE CONCLUSION OF THE MATTER

Throughout this study, we've wrestled with "life under the sun." We've considered the limits of education, work, pleasure, community, justice, and time. We've looked at all the ways we try to derive meaning and purpose—and all the ways we're disappointed.

At this point, it would be easy to simply throw up our hands and surrender to the *hevel* of life. It would be easy to let life take us wherever we want and act on every instinct and impulse, fulfilling every desire. After all, if goodness isn't rewarded under the sun, why even try? Why waste our energy and effort?

Surprisingly, this isn't the Teacher's conclusion or how the Narrator ends Ecclesiastes. Instead, a book that begins in confusion and hopelessness concludes with a message of clarity and hope: Though our days are numbered, God is eternal. While we struggle under the sun, God exists beyond the sun. And from this place beyond the limits, inequities, and confusion, He will act justly. He will reverse *hevel*.

One day, in a way that only God can, every hidden thing will be revealed and accounted for. One day, God will judge between good and evil.

Curiously, the Narrator doesn't tell us when this judgment will happen only that it will happen. It's almost as if time loses meaning when we're speaking of God and His ways. Historically, however, both Jewish and Christian theologians have understood this judgment to come after the resurrection of the dead.

But not knowing the exact timeline doesn't change our hope. Because today, in our struggles and confusion in life under the sun, we trust that God sees and knows. We trust He is taking stock, counting and measuring, and one day, He will reward.

No longer do we count on life under the sun to reward good and punish evil. No longer do we put confidence in our work or efforts to bring us goodness. No longer do we put our hope in youth or our own wisdom. Instead, we trust in God who is beyond the sun. We trust the One who is beyond time itself. And thus trusting, we can rest.

THINK ABOUT IT

When considering God's judgment, do you think of it in negative or positive terms? Explain. Do you understand judgment to include reward? Why or why not? What difference does it make to know that God will reward things that life under the sun does not?

A SABBATH FOR THE PEOPLE OF GOD

While the certainty of God's judgment offers us hope for the future, it also changes the present. It frees us to enjoy the blessings this life can offer.

Look up the following passages and summarize the Teacher's advice about how to live under the sun:

Ecclesiastes 2:24-25

Ecclesiastes 3:12-13

Ecclesiastes 3:22

Ecclesiastes 5:18-19

Ecclesiastes 8:15

Ecclesiastes 9:7-9

SUMMARY

Initially, you may have read these verses as a concession to life's *hevel*—as how to "make the best of things." And to some degree, the Teacher is making peace with life under the sun. He is coming to a workable and livable truce with life's struggles. But this truce is based on his understanding of God's ultimate judgment. Because we have entrusted judgment to God, we use our time under the sun differently. Because we have given over both past and future, we are free to live openly in the present, enjoying whatever goodness God gives us.

In this sense, the Teacher is echoing the promise of the gospel itself: For those who fear God and rest in His protection, there is a release and rest from the *hevel* of life.

READ HEBREWS 4:9-11.

According to verse 10, what must a person do to enter the rest God offers? How does this align with the message of Ecclesiastes?

What could prevent a person from enjoying and receiving the rest God promise (v. 11)? How does this also echo the message of Ecclesiastes?

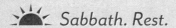 Sabbath. Rest.

You may know the word "sabbath" as a day or period of rest in the Old Testament. Or perhaps you associate it with the Christian practice of setting aside Sunday as "The Lord's Day." But the idea of sabbath is much larger than one day or period of time. Sabbath signals a way of being in the world. To sabbath literally means to cease or stop. Because of its association with work, another synonym is "to rest." The first use of Sabbath in the Scripture occurs in Genesis 2:2 after God has completed His work of creating, "he rested [sabbathed] on the seventh day."

In the context of Ecclesiastes, sabbath includes the idea of stopping work, but it also calls us to cease from the turmoil and weariness of life under the sun. To cease from striving and fighting against *hevel*. To surrender what is outside your control to the One who reigns over all. Hebrews 4:9 explains this same idea in terms of spiritual and eternal rest, describing it as "a Sabbath rest . . . for the people of God." Those who look to God, instead of looking to the *hevel* of this world, can enter into the rest He offers even in this life. It is a rest from trusting in endless labor, endless striving, and endless effort that gets us nowhere. It is the kind of rest that comes when we entrust ourselves fully and completely to Him.

UNEXPECTEDLY GOOD NEWS

CONTINUE IN THE TEXT BY READING HEBREWS 4:12-13.

What helps us understand our own thoughts and motives as we attempt to move to God's rest?

List the parallels you see between Hebrews 4:13 and Ecclesiastes 12:13-14.

Knowing that God will bring everything into judgment can be freeing, but it can also be frightening. We take comfort in knowing good will be rewarded, but what about the evil we do? What about all the times we have been unjust?

CONTINUE IN THE TEXT BY READING HEBREWS 4:14-16.

Why is it important that Jesus both lived under the sun and has passed through the heavens into God's presence?

What is the promise of verse 16?

Ultimately, for the Teacher, the secret to life under the sun was found in remembering what life can and can't give us. Rest from *hevel* comes from confessing our limits and remembering God's limitlessness—including remembering our need of His limitless grace and mercy. So that when we run up against our own injustice, pride, and arrogance, we learn to run to him. Time and time again, in each new season of life, we can run to him confessing our need and surrendering ourselves to His loving hand. Or as Hebrews 4:16 puts it, learning to run to the "throne of grace with boldness, so that we may receive mercy and find grace to help us in time of need."

Until eventually, like the ever-turning earth, we find ourselves ever turning to the One who is beyond the sun.

REFLECTION

Session 8

Below you'll find some questions to help you think through
and apply what you've learned in this week of study.
Be prepared to discuss these if you're doing the study in a group.

1 **Which day of study this week was your favorite and why?**

2 **How would you summarize the Teacher's view of time under the sun?**

3 **How does this compare to what Jesus and the New Testament writers taught about time under the sun?**

4 **What are the main takeaways for you from this week and how do they apply to your life?**

If you're leading the group, check out the leader guide
found at **lifeway.com/lifeunderthesun**.

END NOTES

SESSION 2:

1. Carl Sandberg, "Fog," Poetry Foundation. Accessed May 10, 2023, https://www.poetryfoundation.org/poems/45032/fog-56d2245d7b36c.

2. Tremper Longman III, *The Book of Ecclesiastes* (Grand Rapids, MI: Eerdmans, 1998), 1.

3. Annie Dillard, *Pilgrim at Tinker Creek* (New York: Harper Collins Publishers, 2009), 10.

4. C. S. Lewis, *The Lion, the Witch, and the Wardrobe* (Grand Rapids, MI: Zondervan, 2005), 169.

SESSION 3:

5. Leon Morris, *The Gospel According to John, Revised Edition* (Grand Rapids, MI: Eerdmans, 1995), 106-111.

SESSION 4:

6. A. T. Jebb, L. Tay, L., E. Diener, et al. "Happiness, income satiation and turning points around the world," Nature Human Behavior 2, (2018), 33–38. https://doi.org/10.1038/s41562-017-0277-0.

7. Blaise Pascal, Accessed May 10, 2023, https://www.brainyquote.com/quotes/blaise_pascal_395304.

SESSION 5:

8. Jonathan Glancey, "Gaudi's unfinished Sagrada Familia does not need a completion date." The Guardian September 23, 2011. Accessed May 10, 2023.

9. Dorothy L. Sayers, "Why Work?" in *Letters to a Diminished Church* (Nashville, TN: Thomas Nelson, 2004), 127-128.

10. C T Studd, "Only One Life."

11. Miriam Lichtheim, *Ancient Egyptian Literature: The Late Period, 2nd Ed.* (University of California Press, 2006), 159–180.

SESSION 6:

12. Kathleen Housley, "A Conversation with Jeremy Begbie." *Image Journal, no. 85.* Accessed April 20, 2023. https://imagejournal.org/article/a-conversation-with-jeremy-begbie/.

13. John Donne and John Sparrow, Devotions upon Emergent Occasions, (Cambridge: Cambridge University Press, 2015), 98.

14. Richard C. Davids, *The Man Who Moved a Mountain*, (Philadelphia: Fortress Press, 1970).

SESSION 7:

15. C. S. Lewis, *A Mind Awake: An Anthology of C. S. Lewis*, (Boston, MA: Houghton Mifflin Harcourt, 2003), 37.

16. Blue Letter Bible, "H6663 - ṣāḏaq - Strong's Hebrew Lexicon (csb)." Accessed May 10, 2023, https://www.blueletterbible.org/lexicon/h6663/csb/wlc/0-1/.

17. Blue Letter Bible, "H4941 - mišpāṭ - Strong's Hebrew Lexicon (csb)." Accessed May 10, 2023, https://www.blueletterbible.org/lexicon/h4941/csb/wlc/0-1/.

18. Bethany Hanke Hoang and Kristen Deede Johnson, *The Justice Calling* (Grand Rapids, MI: Brazos Press, a division of Baker Publishing Group, 2017), 19-25.

19. Elizabeth Y. Toomarian and Lindsey Hasak, "Brains Are Bad at Big Numbers, Making It Impossible to Grasp What a Million COVID-19 Deaths Really Means." The Conversation, March 31, 2022. Accessed April 20, 2023. https://theconversation.com/brains-are-bad-at-big-numbers-making-it-impossible-to-grasp-what-a-million-covid-19-deaths-really-means-179081.

20. Elizabeth Woodson, Email to Editor, 6/30/2023.

SESSION 8:

21. Dylan Thomas, "Do not go gentle into that good night," The Poems of Dylan Thomas, (New York: New Directions Publishing, 1971), 207.

22. John Woolford, Daniel Karlin, and Joseph Phelan, Robert Browning: Selected Poems, (Milton Park, Abingdon, Oxon; New York, NY: Routledge, 2013), 652.

23. Margery Williams, *The Velveteen Rabbit*